ABOUT THE AUTHOR

RECOGNIZED AND RESPECTED as one of North America's leading wildlife and natural history photographers, Wayne Lynch has spent the last twenty-five years capturing images of wildlife in wild places the world over. He has photographed both common and unusual creatures in their native habitat in more than fifty countries, travelling extensively for long periods of time and often undergoing considerable physical hardship to get the "perfect shot." His impressive photo credits include hundreds of magazine covers, thousands of calendar shots, and tens of thousands of images published in more than two dozen countries.

Lynch is also an award-winning science writer, a popular guest lecturer, and a veteran photo safari leader. His practical and entertaining approach to natural history, both written and spoken, has attracted the admiration of audiences worldwide.

With an exceptional ability to write for both adults and children, Lynch has authored more than two dozen highly acclaimed natural history books, including *The Great Northern Kingdom: Life in the Boreal Forest*, *Wild Birds Across the Prairies*, *Penguins of the World*, *Mountain Bears*, *Bear:Monarchs of the Northern Wilderness*, *A is for Arctic: Natural Wonders of a Polar World*, and the wildly popular children's book *The Scoop on Poop: The Fascinating Science of How Animals Use Poop*.

Photo credit: Dr. Gordon Court

The curly tops of
blue grama make
it an easy grass to
recognize. It is one
of the common short
grasses of the dry
prairie.

windswept

A PASSIONATE VIEW OF THE PRAIRIE GRASSLANDS

Text and Photography by

WAYNE LYNCH

Assisted by Aubrey Lang

FIFTH
HOUSE

Copyright © 2004 Wayne Lynch
First published by Whitecap Books Ltd. in 1984
Fifth House Ltd. revised/expanded edition first published in 2004

Cover and interior design by Articulate Eye
Edited/copyedited by Geri Rowlatt
Proofread by Meaghan Craven
Scans by St. Solo Computer Graphics

The publisher gratefully acknowledges the support of The Canada Council for the Arts and the Department of Canadian Heritage.

 Canada Council   Conseil des Arts
for the Arts   du Canada

We acknowledge the financial support of the Government of Canada through the Book Publishing Industry Development Program for our publishing activities.

Printed in Canada by Friesens
04 05 06 07 08 / 5 4 3 2 1

First published in the United States in 2004 by Fitzhenry & Whiteside

National Library of Canada Cataloguing in Publication Data

Lynch, Wayne
    Windswept : a passionate view of the prairie grasslands / by Wayne Lynch.

Includes bibliographical references and index.
ISBN 1-894856-25-2

    1. Prairie ecology—North America. 2. Grassland ecology—North America. 3. Natural history—Great Plains. I. Title.
QH541.5.P7L963 2004   577.4'4'097   C2004-900531-6

Fifth House Ltd.   Fitzhenry & Whiteside
A Fitzhenry & Whiteside Company   121 Harvard Avenue,
1511, 1800-4 St. SW   Suite 2
Calgary, Alberta T2S 2S5   Allston, MA 02134

1-800-387-9776
www.fitzhenry.ca

The short-eared owl is a vole and mouse specialist. It nests in a shallow hollow on the ground. When rodents are abundant, it may lay as many as eleven eggs.

CONTENTS

To Aubrey

Whose effervescence is like a spring breeze on the prairies

ACKNOWLEDGMENTS

Ranchers Francis and Myrna Walker, and their children Trevor, Tracey, and Twila, were an important part of my early years on the prairies. They opened their home to me, and I will always remember their warmth and generosity. Others such as Tom Donald and Mel Fitch gave me friendship when I needed it most.

In recent years, many others were generous with their help and encouragement, including, in alphabetical order: affable Marke Ambard, who introduced me to the delights of sex among spadefoot toads; ecologist and friend Dr. J. David Henry and graduate researcher Shelley Pruss, who gave me insight into the swift fox; researcher Janice James, who invited me to wrangle a short-horned lizard; helpful Rick Martin, a biologist with Alberta's Eastern Irrigation District; biologist Dr. Gail Michener, a ground squirrel researcher who graciously endured the compulsions of a photographer; researcher Sandi Robertson, who let me hold a wild Ord's kangaroo rat; Robert Sissons, who invited me to follow him and his burrowing owls; Mark Wendlandt, who acquainted me with the delight and plight of piping plovers; and Pat Young, who made it possible for me to watch big-city peregrines.

Others I wish to thank include the helpful folks at Calgary's Nova Photo, who process my film as if it were their own, and Danny Cheng at Athena Photo Technical Service, who always repairs my broken camera gear in half the time I expect. My good buddy Dr. Gordon Court also deserves mention because of the countless times we laughed and labored together over our cameras. As they would say in New Zealand, he's good value. This is my fifth book with the gang at Fifth House Publishers, and as always, it was painless and fun working with Charlene Dobmeier and Liesbeth Leatherbarrow, freelancers Geri Rowlatt and Meaghan Craven, and designers Brian Smith and Mike McCoy.

Finally, I wish to thank Aubrey Lang, my wife of twenty-nine years. Without her continued enthusiasm and encouragement, my life would certainly have taken a different path. I owe her a debt I can never repay.

PREFACE

I experienced the prairies for the first time in May 1977. It was meant to be a quick weekend exploration of the Frenchman River valley in southwestern Saskatchewan. I never planned to be mesmerized by the effortless drift of a golden eagle across a cloud-cluttered sky, to be surprised by the satin smoothness of a bullsnake as it coiled on my arm, or to be calmed by the liquid song of a meadowlark. Two years later, I abruptly changed careers to work as a science writer and wildlife photographer, and I returned to the comfort of the prairies to begin my life anew. At the time, very little had been written about the natural history of the grasslands, and in 1984, I published *Married to the Wind—A Study of the Prairie Grasslands.* The book was a celebration of the subtle beauty and fascinating biology of one of the most threatened large ecosystems on the planet. I hoped to draw attention to the value and plight of Canada's native grasslands. Sadly, within five years, the book was forgotten, and I moved on to other projects: northern bears, the Arctic, penguins, and the boreal forest. But as everyone knows, first loves are never forgotten, and over the years I returned often to the prairies to refresh my soul with the fragrant scent of grasslands.

Now, twenty years later, it is time again to write about the prairies. I could have written a completely new book, but so much of what I thought was interesting and important in 1984 still is today. Instead, I decided to make a good book better and to build from *Married to the Wind.* I updated and enriched the science in many of the sections, added some completely new ones, and rewrote many to reflect exciting new discoveries in evolutionary and reproductive biology. Whereas *Married to the Wind* was a book about the Canadian grasslands, *Windswept: A Passionate View of the Prairie Grasslands* is much broader in scope and discusses the northern prairie regions of the United States, as well as those in Canada, as they share a common climate, geological history, and wildlife diversity. Photography has always been a vital component of every book I've written, and *Windswept* features fresh new images that reflect my continued fascination with the visual wonder of the prairies and its wildlife. In many cases I purposefully chose photographs of rarely seen wildlife to introduce the reader to the unfamiliar. Join me, as I once again revel in the grasslands—a landscape of promise and surprise.

The pungent aroma of sagebrush is one of the characteristic scents of the prairies. This hardy shrub survives summer droughts and winter blizzards with equal ease.

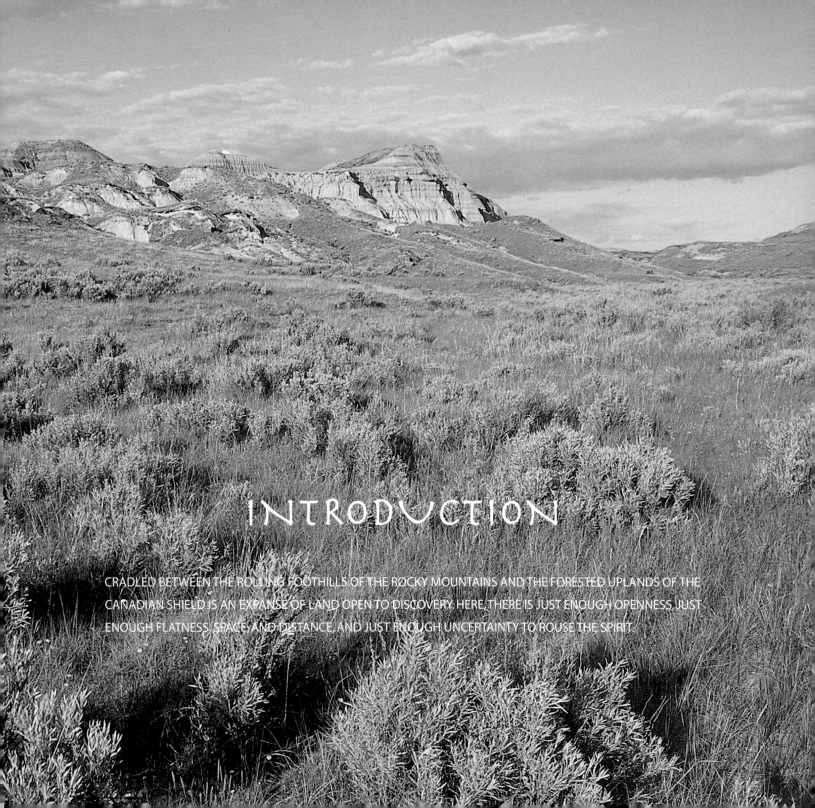

INTRODUCTION

CRADLED BETWEEN THE ROLLING FOOTHILLS OF THE ROCKY MOUNTAINS AND THE FORESTED UPLANDS OF THE CANADIAN SHIELD IS AN EXPANSE OF LAND OPEN TO DISCOVERY. HERE, THERE IS JUST ENOUGH OPENNESS, JUST ENOUGH FLATNESS, SPACE, AND DISTANCE, AND JUST ENOUGH UNCERTAINTY TO ROUSE THE SPIRIT.

Here, there is room to stretch the imagination. It is a land of pulsating life, enticing in its endless moods. It is a place where the amber glow of twilight throws the naked hills into soft relief and where the plaintive call of the curlew drifts from all around. And it is a place where the wind and the pungent smell of pasture sage evoke memories from our unseen past. These are the grasslands.

Grasses have figured prominently in the history of humankind. They nurtured the earliest civilizations that flanked the Tigris and the Euphrates Rivers in Mesopotamia, the Nile River in Egypt, and the Yellow River in China. At that time, 25 to 30 percent of Earth's land surface was cloaked in grass, but the steady encroachment of humans, their cattle, and their plows has reduced that by half. Still, grasses have the widest distribution of any flowering plant on Earth, and grasses of one kind or another can be found on every continent. In South America, the grasslands are called pampas and llanos, those of Eurasia and Africa are called steppes and veldts, respectively, and in North America, the vast grassy expanses are called plains and prairies. Of all the world's grasslands, the quintessential grassland is found in the heart of North America. In its day, the North American plains supported the largest number of grazing animals Earth has ever known: 30 million bison (*Bison bison*), 20 to 30 million pronghorn (*Antilocapra americana*), and millions of elk (*Cervus elaphus*) and mule deer (*Odocoileus hemionus*). Today, though vastly reduced in area, the grasslands of North America are still a wondrous spectacle.

To the casual observer, grass is grass. But within a square meter of grassland there may exist as much variety and complexity as within a hectare of forest. Thus, the North American grassland region is not a vast, uniform sea of grass, but a mosaic of grassland communities that differ in vegetation and wildlife. Within the Great Plains of Canada and the United States, the regional climate, soil, and topography roughly subdivide the grasslands into four separate prairie communities: the tallgrass prairie, the shortgrass prairie, the fescue prairie, and the mixed-grass prairie (see Figure 1).

The tallgrass prairie, sometimes called the true prairie, occupies the eastern edge of the continent's grasslands. It extends from south-central Manitoba to northeastern Texas. For most of its length, the tallgrass prairie separates the deciduous forests in the east from the mixed-grass prairie in the west. The fertility of the tallgrass prairie was its demise, and most of it is now buried under wheat and corn.

The shortgrass prairie is the most arid of the grassland communities. It extends from the Nebraska panhandle south to the high plains of Oklahoma, New Mexico, and Texas. Although there are some intermediate-height grasses present, the dominant grasses are short in stature, such as blue grama (*Bouteloua gracilis*) and needle-and-thread grass (*Stipa comata*).

A third prairie community, the fescue prairie, is limited to Canada, and it forms a cap over the northern edge of the grasslands. The fescue prairie occurs only in Alberta and Saskatchewan and derives its name from the predominance of the grass, rough fescue (*Festuca scabrella*).

The largest grassland community in North America is the mixed-grass prairie, which extends for over

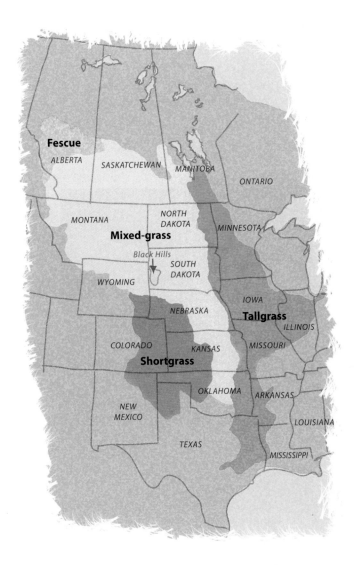

Figure 1 /Distribution of major grasslands types (after Johnsgard 2001).

2,000 kilometers (1,243 mi.) from southern Canada to central Texas and comprises the lion's share of the Central Great Plains of the continent. The northern mixed-grass prairie is the subject of this book. Much of what I will discuss, however, also applies to the southern mixed-grass prairie, as well as the fescue, tallgrass, and shortgrass prairies, since vegetation and wildlife frequently ignore the tidy, convenient scientific limits we set for them.

Within any ecosystem there are subdivisions called *habitats*. Within the northern mixed-grass prairie, it's easy to identify five such habitats: flat to gently rolling grassland plains; sand hill areas; wooded valleys, called coulees; sloughs, the regional term for ponds and potholes; and badlands. I discuss each of these habitats in a separate chapter.

The animals in each habitat may be herbivores (plant eaters), carnivores (meat eaters), or scavengers; in other words, each animal has its own *niche*, or strategy for sustaining itself. Generally, no two species occupy the same niche in a habitat, and commonly they complement each other. A good example of this is shown by the large herbivores of the grasslands. At first, the bison, mule deer, and pronghorn appear to compete for the same niche. On closer examination, we see that the bison is primarily a grazer and prefers to crop grass and sedges. The mule deer is more of a browser, favoring the leaves and buds of shrubs like western snowberry (*Symphoricarpos occidentalis*), saskatoon (*Amelanchier alnifolia*), and red chokecherry (*Prunus virginiana*). The pronghorn is both a browser and a grazer, but is content with less-palatable forage, such as prickly-pear cactus (*Opuntia* spp.), common juniper (*Juniperus communis*), and sagebrush (*Artemisia* spp.). In another instance, when food sources are identical, species may hunt at different times of the day to avoid competition. The red-tailed hawk (*Buteo jamaicensis*) and the great horned owl (*Bubo virginianus*) both prey on the snowshoe hare (*Lepus*

Many of the bison on the northern prairies spent the summer on the mixed-grass plains and then migrated north to the fescue grasslands for the winter.

americanus), but the owl hunts primarily at night and the hawk hunts during the day. Some species fill several niches and live in more than one habitat. For example, the coyote (*Canis latrans*) may feed on plants, animals, or carrion, and it may hunt or forage in all five of the mixed-grassland habitats. These different ways in which a habitat is partitioned permit more complete use of available space and food and encourage the greatest possible diversity of wildlife.

In the grasslands, and elsewhere, plant and animal distribution is not random. Plants and animals inhabit a particular ecosystem, whether it is grasslands, tundra, desert, or forest, because they have certain characteristics or adaptations. The plains prickly-pear cactus (*Opuntia polyacantha*) grows readily in the drier regions of the mixed grasslands because it has certain structural features that lessen water losses and thus minimize its moisture requirements. Charles Darwin and Alfred Russel Wallace were the first to elucidate the theory of evolution by natural selection nearly 150 years ago. Central to the theory are several observations. The first is that creatures produce large numbers of offspring, frequently far in excess of the number that will survive to become breeding adults. For example, a single female wood tick (*Dermacentor andersoni*) may lay 10,000 eggs. Darwin and Wallace also noted that the characteristics of the offspring often varied. From this they reasoned that over millions of years, the number of variations in offspring is astronomical. From the many varieties, the environment selects those that are best suited to survive the prevailing conditions. The survivors leave offspring, thus perpetuating their particular variation. Evolution is primarily a process of selection by the

Richardson's ground squirrels hibernate for the winter, and adult males are the first to surface, usually by the end of February.

environment. As the world evolved, environments changed and the criteria for survival changed. At every step, the existing environment selected (and still does), from among the available variations, those that were best suited for that environment. Knowing this, we can postulate how some creatures became extinct. When the environment changed too quickly, there was insufficient time for successful random variation to arise. These creatures, being unable to dictate the direction of desirable traits, were left to wait for chance genetic change that never came, and the environment passed them by. Thus, in the grassland ecosystem, each and every plant, insect, bird, reptile, and mammal has been selected because of its unique set of characteristics that makes it best suited for that environment.

The earliest European travelers to the prairies came from wooded regions, and they frequently described the prairies in terms of deficiency. The pioneers that followed them were no more insightful; they viewed the prairies as an adversary, to be conquered, controlled, and subdued. They set forth to "tame the West" and "break the land." The "sodbusters" were proud, and so they should have been, for in less than a century, they plowed under two-thirds of the continent's native prairie to assuage the appetite of agriculture. It is an appetite that has not slackened, and every year more native prairies are cultivated for crops or fragmented into depauperate remnants. Humans can be brilliantly destructive when they put their minds to it, and our record with the grasslands attests to that. If we were to chronicle the history of Earth in a book of a thousand pages, each page would cover four and a half million

years. Grasses first appear fifteen pages from the end. In the final five pages, the Central Plains of North America become drier and the grasses expand to form a prairie. Then come humans; their migration from Asia and their occupation of the Americas are crammed into the last word of the book. Somehow, the seventeenth-century arrival of the Europeans, the wholesale slaughter of the bison, the decimation of the Native American culture on the plains, the extermination of the swift fox, prairie wolf, and grizzly, and the destruction of 200 million hectares (494 million acres) of native prairies are telescoped into the final period. Today, the World Wildlife Fund considers the northern prairies to be one of its Global 200 Sites—a natural region of critical conservation concern and one of the most endangered natural habitats in the world.

Our capacity to manipulate the environment has lulled many of us into the belief that we are somehow divorced from the natural community and not subject to its laws. Our calm disregard for the limits of nature and our frequent refusal to accept the universality of natural laws, by which both we and the natural community are governed, may eventually seal the fate of the environment and, ultimately, our own fate.

For decades conservationists have begged for the recognition of the intangible worth of wilderness: scientific, ecological, and aesthetic. Each time we allow an organism to disappear we lose more than genetic diversity; we lose some of our humanity. But until we know what we have, we do not know what we can lose. To understand the grasslands is to know their worth. In the pages that follow, I welcome you to discover the excitement, the diversity, the intricacy, the biology,

and the beauty of the northern prairies. I also hope to transmit a concern for one of the integral components of our continent. To allow the grasslands to disappear would be to sacrifice a landscape that raises the quality of life above mere survival.

The prairie rattlesnake commonly overwinters in rocky crevices or abandoned mammal burrows that penetrate below the frost line and protect it from freezing.

The mushroom outline of a hoodoo betrays the identity of the badlands. For many Native Americans the badlands were a sacred site and the resting place of spirits.

THE LAND ITS FACE AND ITS TEMPERAMENT

ABOVE AND WITHIN EARTH ARE THE FIRES THAT SHAPE OUR WORLD. ABOVE, THE SUN SEETHES AT SEVERAL MILLION DEGREES CENTIGRADE AND DETERMINES OUR GLOBAL CLIMATE THROUGH THE AGENTS OF WIND, RAIN, AND TEMPERATURE. BENEATH US, EARTH'S MOLTEN INTERIOR SIMMERS AT 4,000 DEGREES CENTIGRADE (7,232 DEGREES F.). HEAT FROM THIS INNER FIRE LEAKS TO THE SURFACE AND FRACTURES EARTH'S CRUST INTO PIECES, CALLED *TECTONIC PLATES*, AND THEN SHIFTS THE PLATES ABOUT. FOR BILLIONS OF YEARS BOTH FIRES HAVE BURNED, AND FOR BILLIONS OF YEARS THEY HAVE INFLUENCED THE PRAIRIE REGION.

A fallen aspen leaf interrupts the linear symmetry of a sand flat in the Great Sand Dunes National Monument of southern Colorado.

DRIFTING CONTINENTS AND SPREADING OCEANS

The term *plate tectonics* is used to describe the dual phenomena of moving continents, or continental drift, and seafloor spreading. Starting in 1915, the elaboration of these two phenomena revolutionized the sciences of geology, geophysics, paleontology, and many others.

Overnight, scientists could explain similarities in fossils found on different continents that are separated by thousands of kilometers of open ocean. An understanding of plate tectonics helps to explain a number of features of the mixed-grass prairie region that are evident today. For example, prairie coal and petroleum originated as deposits in tropical seas when North America straddled more southern latitudes. In another instance, the occurrence of thousands of dinosaur fossils in southern Alberta, Montana, and the Dakotas can be explained.

Dinosaurs were reptiles that needed a year-round tropical climate. They could never have survived today's frigid prairie winters, so either the global climate has changed drastically or present-day Alberta and Montana were once located farther south. It seems that both are true, but the drifting of Alberta and Montana over the surface of the earth is the most fascinating to envision. Plate tectonics also explains the global distribution of volcanoes and earthquakes and the mechanisms of mountain building. Though none of these events directly befalls the prairies, the reasons for their absence are an interesting part of the story.

Seventy-five million years of history are exposed in the slopes of the meandering course of the Milk River that flows through Alberta and Montana.

The pincushion cactus blooms in June and grows in the driest areas of the badlands. Its fruits are edible but bland tasting until after the first frost when some people find them sweet and tasty.

Central to the theory of plate tectonics is the notion that Earth's crust, rather than being a continuous layer of rock, is fragmented by heat from its interior into seven major plates and half a dozen minor plates. North America and Greenland are part of the massive North American plate. The western edge of this plate roughly coincides with the Pacific coastline of the continent, while the eastern edge of the plate extends to the middle of the Atlantic Ocean, roughly 3,000 kilometers (1,864 mi.) east of Newfoundland. As in this case, the boundaries of plates do not necessarily coincide with the boundaries of the continents, and many of the plates include both continental and ocean floor crustal sections. The other major tectonic plates are South America, Eurasia, Africa, Australia, Antarctica, and the Pacific.

The plates are in continual motion, shifting and jostling for position. Since they are relatively rigid, most of the action occurs along their edges at the boundaries between adjacent plates. Plates really only do three things: move apart, collide, or slide past each other.

Running down the middle of the floor of the Atlantic Ocean is a ridge of mountains, part of a 59,000-kilometer (36,660-mi.) ridge system that meanders through the Atlantic, Pacific, and Indian Oceans like the seam on a baseball. This oceanic ridge system is an area of seafloor spreading, where adjacent tectonic plates move apart. Along the ridge, molten rock from the underlying mantle of Earth wells up, cools, and hardens and is welded to the edges of the ocean plate on either side of the rift. The newly formed ocean crust then moves away in a continual conveyor-belt fashion. It is no coincidence that the mid-Atlantic Ridge is equidistant from the eastern coast of Canada

and the west coast of North Africa. These lands were once joined, but around 200 million years ago an area of spreading developed between them and has been rafting them apart ever since. At the present rate of seafloor spreading, North America will move west, in your lifetime, a distance roughly equivalent to your height.

If new crust is continually being formed at the oceanic ridge system, then there must be an area where crust is being consumed, or else Earth would gradually increase in diameter. Areas of consumption, called *subduction zones*, occur where tectonic plates collide and form a system of deep ocean trenches. The entire western edge of the Pacific Plate, running through the islands of Japan, the Philippines, and New Zealand, is a subduction zone where the Pacific Plate collides with the Eurasian Plate. Oceanic crust is heavier and denser than continental crust, and the Pacific Plate plunges underneath the Eurasian Plate. As it dips into the trench, it folds, fractures, and eventually melts and is absorbed into the mantle. Earthquakes and volcanoes are the surface manifestations of this crustal digestive process, which explains the frequency of such phenomena throughout the western Pacific. The impact of plates colliding may also thrust the crust up into mountains. Eighty million years ago there was a major subduction zone along the western coast of North America. The oceanic Pacific Plate plunged beneath the continental North American Plate, and, over millions of years, thrust up the Rocky Mountains. The formation of the Rockies was a monumental event for the Central Great Plains. Without the shielding effect of the mountains, the plains would not have become as warm or arid and the grasslands might

Often, a grove of aspen trees is one single organism that is interconnected and shares a common root system. Such aspen clones may be thousands of years old.

A tumbleweed may contain a quarter of a million seeds that it releases as it bounces along. Within thirty years of its introduction into South Dakota in 1877, tumbleweed had spread to most of the northern prairies.

never have developed. Once the mountains formed, weather systems coming from the Pacific had to rise to clear the peaks. As they did, the air cooled and heavy rains resulted, so that the air reaching the prairies on the leeward side of the mountains was robbed of its moisture and had relatively little precipitation to surrender to the grasslands, a phenomenon called the *rain shadow effect.*

The third pattern of tectonic plate movement occurs when plates move parallel to each other. The movement of the plates is not smooth and regular along their edges, and the plates frequently stick. When this happens, pressure builds up until it is sufficient to overcome the resistance and the plates jump back into position. The result is an earthquake. Along the western coast of the United States, the Pacific Plate and the North American Plate are sliding past each other. The San Andreas fault in California marks the junction between these plates and is a notorious earthquake zone.

Continents have repeatedly been fractured and rafted around the globe throughout Earth's four-and-a-half-billion-year history. Climatic conditions on earlier continents differed considerably from today because of differences in the size of the continents and the pattern of ocean currents, but most of all because of changes in the latitudinal position of the continents on the globe. Following the mixed-grass prairie region in its course over the last 600 million years can tell us much about what we see today.

THE PRIMEVAL PLAINS

Six hundred million years ago, life existed only in Earth's oceans. The land itself was barren, lifeless rock. The atmosphere contained little oxygen, but large amounts of carbon dioxide, methane, and ammonium. Lethal ultraviolet rays were just beginning to interact with oxygen to form a protective layer of ozone in the upper atmosphere. The area that was to become the northern prairies straddled the equator, lingering there for over 100 million years. During this time the land was repeatedly inundated by warm, shallow seas, and sediments slowly accumulated at the bottom of these seas. The mixture of rock sediments and sea animal skeletons, compressed over time, created beds of limestone and dolomite. These beds of limestone and dolomite (buried thousands of meters deep) underlie most of the present day mixed-grass prairie and are exposed only in the northern parts of Canada's prairie provinces. Slabs of these ancient rocks, rich in fossil corals and snails, were used to construct the Museum of Natural History, the Legislative building, and university buildings in Regina, Saskatchewan.

In the next phase of its journey, the prairie region moved farther south. Globally, this was a time of great importance, when the first creatures, the ancestors of the scorpions, crawled out of the sea and dared to challenge the land. Plants also made their debut on land, and atmospheric oxygen levels gradually rose as a by-product of photosynthesis.

During the following period, called the Devonian

Period (see Figure 2), the prairie region was driven still farther south and occupied latitudes similar to those of present-day northern Argentina. Cradled between 20 and 40 degrees South latitude, the plains were hot and dry. There were reefs along the edge of the exposed land. The shallow coastal seas, with their tidal flats and lagoons, were subject to high rates of evaporation, which concentrated and precipitated salts into beds of sediments. Today, we recognize these sediments as deposits of potassium chloride, commonly called potash. More than 50 percent of the world's known reserves of potash are located in the mixed-grass prairie region of Saskatchewan.

The Devonian Period continued the evolutionary trends inherited from the preceding periods. As new environments opened up, opportunities for new forms of life arose. The Devonian witnessed the emergence of primitive fish from the sea to begin the invasion and colonization of the land by vertebrates. From these fish evolved amphibians, reptiles, mammals, and eventually the human race.

During the succeeding 65 million years of the Carboniferous Period, the plains retraced their route and returned to equatorial latitudes. Soon afterward, all of the world's continents were driven together by the processes of plate tectonics, forming a super-continent called Pangea. Amphibians were the dominant land animals at this time, but reptiles had become well established; they were poised to take supremacy in the "Age of Dinosaurs."

The immensity of a prairie sky provides an expansive canvas on which the clouds of sunrise can shrink and grow like the heaving of great lungs.

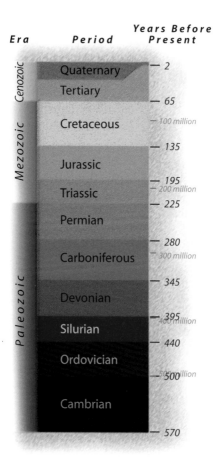

Figure 2 / Geological time scale

THE ORIGINS OF PETROLEUM AND COAL

The super-continent Pangea started to break up about 200 million years ago. The prairie region, along with the rest of North America, was ferried north out of the tropics as the nascent Atlantic Ocean widened under the action of seafloor spreading. En route, the interior plains of North America were again inundated by the sea, this time accumulating deposits of small marine organisms, both plants and animals. The decomposition of such marine organisms produces petroleum. As sediments, which were simultaneously accumulating on the ocean floor, became compacted over time into rocks, the petroleum-forming organisms either were trapped inside and formed oil shales or were squeezed into coarser, more porous rocks that acted as reservoirs. Natural gas settled above the oil.

The Cretaceous Period was the last period in the Age of Dinosaurs, and it ended with the disappearance of these reptilian behemoths whose fossils are found throughout the prairies. The geological sequelae of the Cretaceous Period (65 to 135 million years ago) are readily visible in the mixed-grass prairie. Large amounts of sediments, sometimes 1,000 meters (3,280 ft.) thick, settled out on the bottoms of Cretaceous seas, forming the bedrock that surfaces everywhere throughout the northern prairies. As well, the Cretaceous Period left the prairies with important reserves of coal.

The climate on the northern plains region during the Cretaceous Period was warm and genial, similar to the present climate of Florida. The vegetation was lush, with rich stands of redwoods, palms, ferns, horsetails, and gingkos. In many areas, as the trees died, they fell into loose, boggy soil and shallow pools of stagnant water where the concentration of oxygen was low. The lack of oxygen discouraged bacterial growth, and much of the dead vegetation did not decay completely. This black mass of partially decomposed muck, called peat, was the first stage in the formation of coal. As more trees died and the sediments piled up, the underlying peat became compressed, squeezing out the oxygen and water and resulting in an increase in the percentage of carbon and the production of lignite, the next grade of coal. Further compaction produced a further increase in the percentage of carbon and transformed the lignite into a higher grade of coal, called *bituminous coal*. Finally, if the bituminous coal was subjected to still greater pressure, it was metamorphosed into *anthracite*, the highest grade of coal, with a carbon content of 90 percent. Generally, the higher grades of coal are found at greater depths and are expensive to extract. Seams of bituminous coal are found in the mixed-grass prairie of Alberta.

Near the end of the Cretaceous Period, the prairie region drifted into temperate latitudes that were much the same as today's. In the following 12 million years, more coal was formed, this time from forests of cypress, cedar, magnolia, and chestnut; these latter coal beds are the lignite deposits found in southern Saskatchewan, southwestern Manitoba, eastern Montana, and western North Dakota.

AFTER THE DINOSAURS

The dinosaurs suddenly disappeared 65 million years ago. By then, the Rocky Mountains had begun to form. During the Tertiary Period, which followed the demise of the dinosaurs, there was a general uplift of the continent and the prairie region was never again flooded by the sea. Thus, the exposed land was left to erode. In the ensuing millennia, sediments were scoured and washed down from the newly formed mountains in the west and spread across the prairies. The debris was swept as far east as Manitoba and Minnesota, but it never acquired the great depths nor the extensive coverage of the deposits of the preceding Cretaceous Period.

With the abrupt disappearance of the dinosaurs, numerous ecological vacancies arose. With little or no competition, mammals responded with a rapid expansion of species. The Tertiary Period witnessed the rise of the mammals to dominance, a dominance that persists today. Mammals, with their high, constant body temperature, could be active in all climates, in all seasons, and at any hour of the day. This was in sharp contrast to the previously reigning reptiles, which were seriously restricted in their mobility by their dependence on the heat of the sun. Mammals also provided their offspring with special care, a characteristic that was virtually nonexistent in the reptiles. The mammals gave their young milk, grooming, protection, and instruction, all of which increased the likelihood of survival. Natural selection had chosen again, and the mammals were the winners.

THE ICE AGE

The present Ice Age began approximately 2 million years ago. Controversy still exists about how often the ice advanced, what starts an Ice Age, and whether there will be another, but speculation, disagreement, and controversy have always been integral elements of science and part of its appeal.

Glaciers presently cover 10 percent of Earth's land surface, most of them found in Greenland and Antarctica. During the height of the last glaciation, roughly 15,000 years ago, nearly a third of Earth's land surface was laden with ice. The glaciers grew when more snow fell in the winter than melted in summer. As the depth of snow increased, the snow became compacted into ice. The deepest layers were subjected to the greatest pressures, and they began to flow. As the glaciers grew in height, they exerted an influence on the regional weather; they began to behave like mountains. Weather systems, driven by the predominantly southwesterly winds, rose when they met the glacial mounts. As the air rose, it cooled and released its moisture in the form of snow. In this way, the southern lip of the glaciers thickened while their northern edges thinned. The glaciers crept slowly south.

Several centers of glaciation—Keewatin, Ungava, and Baffin Island—merged to create the massive Laurentide Ice Sheet that engulfed the greater part of central and eastern Canada. At its center, over present-day Hudson Bay, the ice sheet may have been over 4 kilometers (2.5 mi.) thick. Along its southern lip, the ice sheet was much thinner, and the glacier never extended much beyond the Canada–United States border.

The present Ice Age has not been a protracted, uninterrupted occupation of the land, but rather a series of successive episodes in which the ice sheet grew and covered the land, then melted and retreated. Geologists call these episodes "glacial" and "interglacial" periods, respectively. We are now living in an interglacial period. Specialists generally agree that glaciers have descended upon the prairie region at least four times since the start of the current Ice Age. These four glacial advances, starting with the last and most recent one, are called the Wisconsin, Illinoian, Kansan, and Nebraskan Glaciations. (To remember the sequence, try using "Will the Ice Keep North?" The initial letter of each of the main words matches those of the glacial advances.) Each glacial advance tended to erase the handiwork of previous episodes, and in the prairies, the visible glacial effects are primarily those of the Wisconsin Glaciation, which started to retreat between 15,000 and 18,000 years ago. By 12,000 years ago, the mixed-grass prairie region was free of ice.

CAUSES OF GLACIATION

Central to a discussion of glaciation is an explanation of its causes. Glaciers grow when the mean global temperature drops. A drop of only 3 to 4 degrees Centigrade (5 to 7 degrees F.) would have been all that was necessary to start the glaciers of northern Canada growing and moving. The presence of an ice field in itself will cause the temperature to drop. The age-old dilemma of which came first, the chicken or the egg, is immediately apparent. But recent findings have proven influential in solving the dilemma.

The recent Ice Age, which started some 2 million years ago, is not the first to befall Earth. Major Ice Ages occurred 450 million years ago and then again 300 million years ago. Alfred Wegener, the scientific heretic who, ninety years ago, dared to propose that continents drift, noted quite early that the occurrence of major Ice Ages coincided with the presence of continents in polar latitudes. For example, during the last Ice Age in the Carboniferous Period, some 300 million years ago,

a large ice mass covered Antarctica and India and parts of South America, Africa, and Australia when these continents were clustered over southern polar latitudes. Currently, two-thirds of Earth's land mass rides north of the equator, with clustering in the polar latitudes. It is speculated that the presence of continents in northern latitudes reduces the effectiveness of ocean circulation in distributing warm, tropical currents to polar regions and, consequently, leads to an overall reduction in global temperatures.

There are other factors that also influence global temperatures. The amount of surface ice and snow on Earth determines the amount of solar reflection and adsorption and thus has an influence on world temperatures. Another factor may be volcanic ash spewed into the atmosphere, which intercepts the sun's rays and so may lower the temperature of the planet.

If the position of the continents predisposes Earth to an Ice Age, are there other factors that determine the timing of glacial and interglacial periods within an Ice Age? Milutin Milankovitch, a brilliant Serbian mathematician, proposed a theory to explain how it happens. His theory, which today we call the Milankovitch cycles, poses that three variables affect the amount of solar radiation heating Earth's surface. First, the shape of Earth's orbit around the sun varies from more elliptical to more circular over a period of 100,000 years. Then, there is the tilt of Earth on its axis, which varies from 22 degrees to 24.5 degrees every 41,000 years. And finally, there is the wobble of Earth on its axis, which has a 23,000-year cycle. All three factors combine to determine how much of the sun's heat reaches Earth's surface.

In the final analysis, the causes of glaciation are many, likely acting in consort. Though all of the factors mentioned may be involved, the latitudinal position of the continents seems to be the first prerequisite for the development of an Ice Age. The last Ice Age in the Carboniferous Period lasted for at least 50 million years, until the continents shifted and moved toward the equator. This being the case, it appears that we are locked into another Ice Age, and we can expect glacial periods to recur repeatedly until the continents again drift to less-polar latitudes.

GLACIERS SHAPE THE PRAIRIE LANDSCAPE
Though the causes of the Ice Age are speculative, the effects are not. The effects of the Ice Age fall into two main categories: depositional and erosional. Each left its mark on the northern mixed-grass prairie.

As the tongues of ice moved across the prairies, they churned up fine and coarse rock, which became imbedded in their undersurfaces. Additional rocks piled in front of the ice and along its sides as the glaciers pushed forward like highway graders forging a path. Within any given area, the leading edge of the glacier was constantly shifting, with minor retreats and advances. When the glacier melted and withdrew, the rock it had nosed along was deposited as distinct mounds, called *end moraines*. Elsewhere, fragments of ice would break free, stagnate, and melt, depositing their load of gravel and sand. At other times, the receding glacier left a veneer of unsorted rocky rubble, the cargo it had carried in its undersurface. Across the breadth of the northern prairies these glacial events were repeated and erased innumerable times. When

the ice left for the final time, the bedrock of the plains was hidden, obscured beneath an uneven blanket of sand, silt, gravel, and boulders up to 150 meters (492 ft.) thick. This irregular cover of glacial debris determined the final topography of the northern prairies and created the characteristic rolling terrain.

Glacial debris contains not only ground-up rocky material derived from the local bedrock, but also many large and small rocks plucked from the granite of the Canadian Shield by the glacier and transported hundreds of kilometers south. These far-traveled rocks, called erratics, litter the northern prairies. Many erratics are quite large and served as scratching posts for the bison. In the treeless plains, the boulders were a welcome occurrence, especially in spring when the shaggy beasts shed their heavy winter coats. Over the centuries the boulders were polished smooth, each in the center of a hollow dug by thousands of hooves. The rubbing stones of the bison can still be spotted throughout the mixed-grass prairie, haunting reminders of days long-gone, when bison still roamed the plains.

The normal drainage of the land in the northern prairies is to the east and the north. As the glaciers melted they retreated in a northeasterly direction, forming a barrier to the normal drainage of the land, so that water ponded between the glacier and the higher ground in the west. The ponded water formed glacial lakes that filled with sediment up to 6 meters (19.7 ft.) thick. The flat, silt and clay bottoms of Rosetown, Indian Head, and Regina Lakes were to become the prime wheat-growing areas of Saskatchewan. The glacial lakes of Saskatchewan and Manitoba tended

The appeal of Red Rock Coulee in southern Alberta is the numerous sandstone concretions, some of which are 2 meters (6 ft.) across.

to spread out and cover large areas. Lake Agassiz, which formed in central and southern Manitoba, was the largest of all the glacial lakes and possibly the largest lake of any type that Earth has ever known. In southern Alberta, the land has greater relief; there, the glacial lakes tended to be long and narrow and occupied river valleys. The lakes were more transient than those of Saskatchewan and Manitoba, and sediments had less time to accumulate. There were glacial lakes in Alberta near Lethbridge and Drumheller.

The meltwater that fed the glacial lakes spewed from the bottom of glaciers loaded with sand, gravel, silt, and clay. The coarser material, sand and gravel, settled first into broad, fan-shaped outwash plains immediately adjacent to the glacier, while the finer silt and clay particles stayed suspended in the meltwater and later settled in the glacial lakes. Today, the outwash plains form porous ground cover that often serves as underground reservoirs of water, called *aquifers*.

We've now covered the three kinds of deposits found on the mixed-grass prairie: those left by the glacier itself, those formed on the bottoms of glacial lakes, and those spread by meltwater. By keeping in mind the fragment size of the deposits, and when and how the deposits accumulated, we can look at any fairly flat area in the mixed-grass prairie and differentiate between a field of glacial debris, an old glacial lake bed, and an outwash plain. Deposits derived directly from the glacier itself are an unsorted jumble of rocky debris. This is the ground cover where erratics are most commonly found. This is also the most rolling of the three landscape deposits, and depressions are frequently occupied by sloughs. Glacial lakes form after a glacier has left an area, and their fine sediments of clays and silts mask any previous rocky deposits. Old lake beds, then, have few visible rocks, are very level, and are frequently cultivated because of the high water-holding capacity of clay. Outwash plains, on the other hand, are composed of coarser sediment, often sand, deposited by flowing water. The water sorts the sediments so that the deposits are of uniform particle size. The porous nature of outwash plains normally precludes accumulation of surface water as sloughs and makes them less attractive for agriculture.

In the erosional category of Ice Age effects, melting ice is again responsible. We have already seen that in the early phase of glacial departure from the prairies, the ice blocked the normal northeast drainage route. Consequently, glacial meltwater, as well as glacial lake spillways, coursed in a southerly direction and ultimately drained into the Mississippi River. The running water stripped away the glacial deposits and ate into the bedrock, carving out deep impressive valleys. The dramatic Milk River valley and the valleys of the Red Deer, Missouri, and Frenchman Rivers are examples of old meltwater channels. Today, these rivers are a shadow of their former size. The Frenchman River in southern Saskatchewan, for instance, is a mere 10 meters (33 ft.) wide, but it flows along the bottom of a broad valley that is several kilometers wide in some areas and from 30 to 100 meters (98 to 328 ft.) deep. In southern Alberta, a whole series of dry-bottomed valleys etch the landscape. Whiskey Gap, Etzikom Coulee, Chin Coulee, and Forty Mile Coulee are former meltwater channels created when the glacier relinquished its grip and withdrew from the land.

THE ARRIVAL OF HUMANS

Though the Ice Age is best known for its erosional and depositional effects on the landscape, the Ice Age affected the land in yet another way: it paved the way for the coming of humans. With vast quantities of Earth's water locked in ice, global sea levels dropped.

A drop of 50 meters (164 ft.) would have been all that was necessary to expose the submarine plateau spanning Alaska and Siberia. However, at the height of the last glaciation, the Wisconsin, global sea levels dropped more than 100 meters (328 ft.), creating an expansive 1,500-kilometer (932-mi.) wide land bridge between Asia and America. The migration began. Early humans probably followed herds of game that also moved across the bridge from Siberia to Alaska. The immigrants included bison, deer, mammoths (*Mammuthus* spp.), and mastodons (*Mammut americanum*), and with them their predators: sabertooth tigers (*Smilodon* spp.), lions (*Panthera leo*), bears (*Ursus arctos*), wolves (*Canis lupus*), and humans. Camels (*Camelops* spp.) and horses (*Equus* spp.) moved in the opposite direction, from Alaska to Siberia. It is uncertain how long humans have been in North America, but some estimates date back to 40,000 years ago. The earliest stone tools come from the Yukon and are 27,000 years old. But no matter when it was that humans first arrived on the continent, their presence on the northern prairies 12,000 years ago is unquestionable. Then, migrating at an easy 15 kilometers (9.3 mi.) per year, they might have reached Panama in just 600 years. Practically overnight, in the time scale of Earth, humans moved from immigrant hunters to masters of a continent.

POSTGLACIAL FORESTS

Early humans on the northern prairies hunted mainly in forests, not grasslands. The grasslands had been bullied south into the southern United States by the frigid advance of the glacier. When the Laurentide Ice Sheet was at its maximum extent during the Wisconsin Glaciation, straddling the international border, a spruce

An ancient tepee ring overlooks the Frenchman River Valley in southern Saskatchewan. The elevated site would have been a perfect one from which to locate migrating herds of bison.

forest extended from near the ice margin south into Kansas. As the glacier slowly retreated, the forest followed. Tree stumps and other remains of these past postglacial forests are occasionally unearthed when ditches are dug. Close on the heels of the retreating forests were the grasslands. By 8,000 to 10,000 years ago, the glacier had withdrawn far enough north to restore warmer and drier conditions to the northern prairie region, and the grasslands returned.

PRAIRIE CLIMATE

Climate has always been the principal factor determining the distribution of vegetation, and it was the climate that orchestrated the postglacial return of the grasslands to the northern prairies. The climate of today's mixed-grass prairie is a cool, semi-arid one, characterized by extremes. In winter, temperatures may plunge to -40 degrees Centigrade (-40 degrees F.), forcing rocks to wince, and in summer, the mercury can climb to an intolerable +40 degrees Centigrade (104 degrees F.). These seasonal extremes occur because of the interior location of the prairies. Oceans, with their voluminous heat-holding capacity, moderate the climate of coastal regions, but the centers of continents enjoy no such amelioration. In Swift Current, Saskatchewan, one of the coldest regions of the mixed-grass prairie, the average maximum January temperature is -18 degrees Centigrade (0 degrees F.). At the same latitude on the coast of British Columbia, the average maximum for the same month is +2 degrees Centigrade (36 degrees F.). Farther south, the temperature differences are less extreme. For example, in Casper, Wyoming, the maximum January

temperature is 2 degrees Centigrade (36 degrees F.), whereas the coast of Oregon enjoys January maximums of 12 degrees Centigrade (54 degrees F.).

Extremes in temperature are also a daily pattern. The humidity of the prairies is low, and with little water vapor and few clouds to block the heating rays of the sun, daytime temperatures can easily climb. At night, again because of the low humidity, there is little moisture in the air to stall the cooling of Earth, and air temperatures drop. The low humidity, however, gives the northern prairie region more hours of sunshine than most regions except the desert southwest.

Lying in the rain shadow of the Rocky Mountains, the precipitation on the northern prairies averages from 30 to 40 centimeters (12 to 16 in.), with half of the moisture falling between April and July and a quarter of it falling as snow. But an average is just that, and yearly precipitation levels can swing between 10 centimeters (4 in.) and 60 centimeters (24 in.). In Canada, the driest regions of the mixed-grass prairie are the adjacent corners of southern Alberta and southern Saskatchewan. From this point, the precipitation increases to the north, the west, and the east. During the lean years, the specter of drought returns and, with it, memories of the 1930s. From 1930 to 1939, there was progressively less rain each year until 1937. The dust blew and crops failed. Farmers squinted into the sun for a hint of respite. But the temperament of the prairies is written in stone, and the hopes and dreams of humans have never changed it for an instant.

Winds add another dimension to the character of the prairies. Cowboys advise not to exert yourself if your hat blows away, just sit for a while and grab the next one that rolls by. The mixed-grass prairie is flushed by winds from the west that blow strongest from March to May. The dry winds tug at the moisture in plants and soil. Though the prairies receive 30 to 40 centimeters (12 to 16 in.) of moisture annually, the evaporation rate may exceed that three times over, making the area more arid than expected. In winter, warm, desiccating winds, called *chinooks*, can sweep down the eastern slopes of the Rockies and raise the temperature by many degrees in a matter of minutes, providing a welcome reprieve from the icy grip of the season. The winds and temperature changes are usually strongest near the mountains, gradually lessening as they move east. Legendary chinooks also occur in the Black Hills of South Dakota, which holds the record for the fastest rise in temperature ever recorded. In January 1943, the temperature rose 27 Centigrade degrees (49 F. degrees) in just two minutes. The snow-eating temperatures persisted for several hours, then suddenly plummeted back down to -20 degrees Centigrade (-4 degrees F.), dropping 32 Centigrade degrees (58 F. degrees) in just twenty-seven minutes!

MICROCLIMATE

On a typical day in May when the weather forecaster reports clear skies and a temperature of 25 degrees Centigrade (77 degrees F.), a person knows what to expect. But on the same day, the conditions will be dramatically different on the clay slopes of the badlands, on the grassy tops of a butte, or beneath the shaded shrubbery of a coulee. In each of these areas, soil moisture, humidity, wind velocity, sunlight, and temperature vary, and they combine to create a whole spectrum of "mini" climates, or microclimates. It's the microclimate that concerns wildlife and also determines the fine features of plant distribution. Let's consider a number of aspects of microclimates in detail. North-facing slopes, for example, are consistently cooler and suffer less evaporation than slopes that face south, and slopes in general retain less moisture and experience higher rates of runoff than level areas. Because of wind, elevated areas are cooler than depressions in summer, and they experience less frost damage in spring and autumn.

The vegetation, as well as the topography, has an effect on the microclimate. The foliage of plants protects the ground against extremes of temperature, reduces the velocity of the wind (and thus the drying effects), and adds moisture to the air through the respiration of its leaves.

Because of all of these factors, animals, especially small ones, have a variety of microclimates from which to choose, and they frequently vary their selection with the seasons. Plants are also influenced by the characteristics of microclimates. For example, any hill in the mixed-grass prairie may be vegetated by a different set of grasses, wildflowers, and shrubs on each of its four sides—the plants capitalizing on the subtle differences in soil, sunlight, temperature, and moisture.

The five different habitats of the mixed-grass prairie result primarily from five different microclimates. The different microclimates dictate which plants and animals are present in each habitat. The next chapter deals with the most extensive of the five prairie habitats, the level plains.

The gently rolling topography of the northern prairies is a consequence of glacial scouring.

THE LEVEL PLAINS FLAT ALL YEAR ROUND

OF THE FIVE HABITATS IN THE MIXED-GRASS PRAIRIE, THE LEVEL PLAINS ARE MOST FAMILIAR. IT'S A SOFT, EASY LANDSCAPE, FLAT OR GENTLY RUFFLED INTO WAVES OF ROLLING HILLS. HERE, THE SUN AND CLOUDS FINGER THE LAND WITH LIGHT AND SHADOW AND CHANGE ITS CHARACTER BY THE MINUTE, AND EVERYWHERE THERE IS GRASS WITH A PEACEFUL GRIP ON THE LAND.

THE NATURE OF GRASS

Grasses evolved some 60 million years ago from tropical, woody ancestors, of which the bamboo is a present-day example. The tenacity and resilience of grasses have enabled them to tackle frigid tundra, searing sand dunes, rarefied alpine slopes, marshes, swamps, and deserts. But grasses reach their greatest luxuriance and diversity in the grasslands of the world. Worldwide, there are over 9,000 species of grasses, with 300 or more of these growing in the northern mixed-grass prairies. Grasses are commonly divided into shortgrasses, less than 0.5 meters (1.6 ft.) tall, mid-grasses, 0.5 to 1.5 meters (1.6 to 5 ft.) tall, and tallgrasses, 1.5 to 3.0 meters (1.6 to 9.8 ft.) tall. The mixed-grass prairie is composed of species from all three groups, although shortgrasses and mid-grasses dominate; the final blend is dictated by precipitation. In the moister peripheral regions of the mixed-grass prairie, mid-grasses dominate, and in years of above-average precipitation, they may flourish throughout the entire region. In normal years, the shortgrasses, such as blue grama (*Bouteloua gracilis*), grow in the driest sections of the region but become more widespread in years of drought. In successive years of drought, many of the mid-grasses may die and take decades to return.

Grass can be trampled, buried, broken, or burnt, and still it comes back. Natural selection has honed it to endure. Grasses have a highly branched root system that absorbs moisture from the most miserly shower—a beneficial adaptation in the semi-arid climate of the mixed-grass prairie. In a famous experiment conducted in the

An oak tree in North Dakota valiantly makes a foothold in the grassy prairies. Recurrent wildfires normally kill many seedlings long before they reach such a size.

Foxtail barley, one of the most beautiful of grasses, tolerates flooding and alkaline soils, and commonly grows around sloughs and along waterways.

With so little precipitation in the prairies, the freezing temperatures of winter may precede any snowfall and transform the surface of sloughs into sheets of silver.

1930s, a single rye grass plant (*Elymus* spp.) produced 620 kilometers (384 mi.) of roots in just four months. When the plant's 15 billion root hairs (the fine structures through which water and minerals are absorbed) were included, the total length was four times the distance from Calgary, Alberta, to Dallas, Texas, and the surface area equaled that of two basketball courts.

The astonishing root density of grass plants holds the soil in place and protects the land against erosion. Such root density also enabled the prairie settlers of the late 1800s to cut the soil into building blocks and construct homes of sod. The sod houses provided good protection against the winter cold, the summer heat, and the year-round wind,

In view of Montana's Sweetgrass Hills, a pregnant mule deer moves to the shelter of a familiar coulee where it will soon give birth.

but rain was another matter. Pioneers joked that if it rained outside for a day, it would rain inside for two.

Grasses have hollow stems strengthened by solid nodes, or knobs, which enable the plants to bend in the wind without breaking. Even if a grass plant is trampled, the tissue on the lower side of the nodes can elongate and straighten the plant back up toward the light.

Because of their thrifty management of water, grasses do well in regions of low rainfall. The leaves of grasses have a thick surface layer that resists evaporation, and their pores, through which carbon dioxide and oxygen are exchanged, are recessed in grooves along the leaf surface, which further lessens the drying effects of the wind. Some grasses have additional protection against desiccation. For example, the leaves of northern wheat grass (*Agropyron dasystachyum*) and western wheat grass (*A. smithii*) have large, thin-walled cells on the leaf surface. These lose water more readily than usual surface cells so when the plant is water stressed, the loss of turgor in these large cells causes the leaves to roll into a tight tube. This effectively reduces the surface areas of the leaf that are exposed to the drying effects of the wind. Without this mechanism, the grass plant would just wilt.

A grass blade grows from its base rather than its tip; thus, it can be cropped by grazing animals and still continue to grow. Also, the critical growing parts of the grass plant are located at the ground surface, or below, and this protects the plant from fire. This last characteristic helped to maintain, and possibly expand, the mixed-grass prairie region over the last 10,000 years. The Native Americans of the plains routinely ignited the prairies in warfare and hunting. These recurrent fires were devastating to shrubs and trees attempting to secure a foothold in the grasslands, and this perpetuated the dominance of the more fire-resistant grasses. Grasses rebounded quickly after every fire.

PRAIRIE WILDFLOWERS

Though different species of grasses comprise greater than 80 percent of the vegetation of this land, dozens of varieties of wildflowers color the prairie landscape. In the north, the purple prairie crocus (*Anemone patens*) is usually the first wildflower to bloom, typically about the middle of April. Some plains Native peoples believed that the crocus was more than a portent of spring; it was an opportunity for reflection. When a hunter found his first flower of the year he would light his pipe and sit nearby. After ceremoniously anointing the earth, the sky, and the four compass points, he would contemplate his past and future life. After a period of peaceful introspection he would reverently empty the ashes from his pipe beside the flower and continue his journey, heartened by the experience.

The early blooming wildflowers benefit from the moisture left by the melted snow, but they must also contend with the unpredictable and frequently cool spring temperatures. As a consequence, many of these species, including moss phlox (*Phlox hoodii*) and silverweed (*Potentilla anserina*), grow in clusters close to the ground, creating their own microclimate. Somewhat sheltered from the chilling winds of spring, temperatures within these clusters of flowers may be 5 Centigrade degrees (9 F. degrees) higher than the surrounding air. The prairie crocus uses a different strategy to warm itself—it follows the sun. Throughout the day, crocus flowers track the course of the sun, and the disk shape of their blossoms functions like a miniature disk antenna, focusing the sun's heat onto the centers of the flowers. After a cool night in April, the fuzzy stamens of the crocus flower are frequently crowded with beetles, bees, and flies. The insects are attracted by the warmer microclimate, which can be more than 10 Centigrade degrees (18 F. degrees) warmer than the chilly morning air. In the process, the insects benefit the flower by inadvertently pollinating it.

As the months progress, the flowers in bloom become taller and taller in order to compete with the growing grasses for light. By late summer, only the tallest flowers, such as asters (*Aster* spp.), goldenrods (*Solidago* spp.), and sunflowers (*Helianthus* spp.), are still in bloom.

FLOWERS TALK TO INSECTS

For centuries, flowers have inspired painters and poets, and their petals have sometimes helped me to determine whether I was loved or not, but these are not their reasons for being. Flowers talk to insects.

Flowers contain both female and male parts in the center of their blossoms. Although some flowers can pollinate, or fertilize, themselves, in most instances a pollen grain (the male cell) from one plant unites with the ovule (the female cell) from another plant. This union produces a seed. Flowers face a problem in achieving this union since they are anchored by their roots to separate spots. The solution is a ménage à trois, with insects or the wind as the third partner. (In other ecosystems, birds and bats may also serve as pollinators.) To attract the different insects, flowers have evolved specialized structures, colors, odors, and nectar glands. Generally, each flower tries to attract only a few specific pollinators, and among prairie flowers there are bee flowers, moth flowers, fly flowers, and wind flowers.

Typically, flowers that attract bees are brightly colored in blues and yellows, and they have a sweet

Golden-bean is a common wildflower of May and early June. It is a poisonous member of the legume family.

fragrance. The petals of these flowers are arranged to provide a convenient landing platform, and the nectar glands at the base of the petals reward the bee. Since bees are diurnal, many of these flowers close at night. Among others, the low larkspur (*Delphinium bicolor*) and wild mint (*Mentha arvensis*) are good examples of bee flowers.

Moth flowers are invariably white and heavily scented to attract their nocturnal pollinators. Moths use their long tongues to reach the sweet nectar glands and usually do not settle during feeding, so the flowers they pollinate do not need special landing platforms. The hedge bindweed (*Convolvulus sepium*) and gumbo evening-primrose (*Oenothera caespitosa*) are moth flowers.

Flies are usually not attracted by sight, but by smell, and many flies are attracted by the smells of dung, humus, and carrion. The prairie carrion flower (*Smilax herbacea*) has small, dull greenish white blossoms that lure flies with the odor of death.

Finally, there is the large group of flowers that relies on the wind for pollination. Wind pollination was the first pollination strategy to evolve in plants millions of years ago. Today, it still provides a vital service to many of the flowering plants of the grasslands. Wind-pollinated flowers have no need for bright colors, sugary nectar glands, enticing smells, or fancy landing platforms. Most have no petals at all, as they would only act as a barrier to windborne pollen. Grasses, the dominant flowering plants of the prairies, are married to the wind, for all are pollinated by it. Indeed, grass flowers are so dull and inconspicuous that it surprises many people to learn that grasses have flowers at all.

Wildlife frequently ignores the neat, tidy categories that scientists contrive, and insect pollinators are no exception. Any given flower may be visited by beetles, butterflies, bees, and flies, and any one of these may accidentally pollinate the flower. This does not invalidate what has been said about the various pollination strategies of prairie flowers; it merely illustrates that the system is a flexible one.

SEEDS ON THE MOVE

Prairie grasses and wildflowers rely on the wind, birds, mammals, and insects for another function: to disperse their seeds. In autumn, the wind plucks countless Russian thistles (*Salsola kali*), or tumbleweeds, from their moorings and sends them wandering across the level plains of the northern prairies. They cluster for a while in hollows and stack against fences, but when the wind changes direction, they are whipped into motion again. Each tumbleweed contains about 250,000 seeds, which it releases as it bounces along. The Russian thistle was accidentally introduced into South Dakota in 1877, and within thirty years it had spread to prairie Canada and more than a dozen states, an eloquent testimonial to the efficiency of the wind as a dispersal agent.

Birds and animals may also help prairie plants spread their seeds around. Grass seeds can stick to the muddy feet of wading birds and be transported from one slough to another. The famous evolutionist Charles Darwin broke apart a 170-gram (6-oz.) ball of mud from the leg of a gray partridge (*Perdix perdix*), an introduced prairie game bird, and carefully watered the dirt. Eighty-two seedlings, of five species, sprouted, convincing proof that birds are good at moving seeds around. Even seeds that are ingested may survive. Viable seeds have been recovered from bird droppings more than five days after they were eaten, and in five days, a migrating bird, such as a bobolink (*Dolichonyx oryzivorus*), may fly thousands of kilometers.

Many seeds possess barbs and hooks that can catch on fur and feathers and get a free ride. The seeds of porcupine grass (*Stipa spartea*) and needle-and-thread grass are barbed and easily hook on fur. Other animals, such as Ord's kangaroo rats (*Dipodomys ordii*), may gather and cache seeds, which are later forgotten and sometimes germinate.

ANTS AND HOPPERS

Some insects also disperse seeds, and none is more conspicuous than the industrious ant. Ants are social insects that cannot survive alone. All are members of a colony in which there are three standard castes: fertile males, fertile females, and sterile female workers. The workers come in different sizes, depending upon whether they guard the colony, gather food, or stay inside the nest doing housework. In late spring or early summer, when conditions are right within the colony, winged male and female ants are hatched and raised. Then, in response to environmental cues such as specific temperatures or rainfall, the winged ants fly from the nest. Ants from many colonies in an area may emerge at the same time, swarm together, and mate. In this way, ants establish new colonies. The males die shortly after their courtship flights, but the mated females fly off alone, dig a small, sheltered chamber in the soil, and lay their eggs. The founding female, called the queen, soon sheds her wings,

The thick white juice that oozes from broken stems and leaves give the milkweed its common name. Each ripe seed pod contains about fifty seeds.

and the large muscles that she used for her nuptial flight are resorbed to provide nutrition to sustain her until her first brood of eggs hatches. The new hatchlings develop into workers which then feed her.

Ants intrigue people because they seem to display many human qualities, such as sociability, industriousness, and allegiance. In the mixed-grass prairie there are dozens of ant species, and, like people, they make their living in a variety of ways. They hunt, harvest, herd, enslave, and conquer.

Carnivorous ants (*Formica* spp.) are the most common type of ants on the prairies. They hunt and devour caterpillars, beetles, weevils, and termites. If the prey is large and struggles, they can immobilize it by spraying formic acid from a gland at the tip of their abdomen. Another group of ants, the harvester ants (*Pogonomyrmex* spp.), builds conspicuous mounds, and they can be distinguished from all other prairie ants by their long waist. Harvester ants collect seeds, which they first coat with saliva that has antibiotic properties and then store in underground granaries, sometimes 5 meters (16 ft.) below the surface. Harvester ants fastidiously clip the vegetation from around their mounds, and it is speculated that this prevents root channels from developing into the underlying granaries, which would allow water to seep in and spoil the grain.

One of the most conspicuous ants on the northern prairies is the red-and-black thatching ant (*Formica obscuripes*). It also builds large mounds, up to 1 meter (3 ft.) tall, similar in shape to those of harvester ants, but it covers the domes with tiny twigs and bits of dried grass. A colony of thatching ants may contain a quarter million inhabitants. The thatching ant is sometimes a hunter and sometimes a herder. Thatching ants herd clusters of aphids, jokingly called "ant cows." Aphids are tiny insects that gorge themselves by sucking sap and juices from the stems and leaves of plants. The sap is converted into a sugar-rich honeydew. Thatching ants "milk" the aphids by stroking them with their antennae, which induces them to excrete a sweet drop of honeydew from their rear end that the ants suck up. Not surprisingly, the ants are very attentive to the aphids and protect them from predators, such as the ubiquitous seven-spotted ladybug (*Coccinella septempunctata*).

Other prairie ants in the genus *Formica* display characteristics reminiscent of the darker side of humankind. Some are slave makers that steal eggs from other colonies, and when the captured eggs hatch, the ants are used as workers. Another tactic practised by thatching ants (*F. obscuripes*) in some areas is for the queen to invade the nest of another species and kill the resident queen. The conquering queen then lays her own eggs, which are cared for by the "host" workers. Eventually, the conquerors outnumber their subjects and a pure colony of thatching ants results.

The ants of the prairies may be easy to overlook because of their diminutive size and silence, but prairie grasshoppers are often impossible to ignore as they explode underfoot in noisy, buzzing flight. Well over a hundred species of grasshoppers occur in the northern prairies, and in some years, a few species, including the clear-winged grasshopper (*Camnula pellucida*) and the lesser migratory grasshopper (*Melanoplus sanguinipes*), can multiply into prodigious numbers. Most grasshoppers lay their eggs in late summer and early autumn. The females repeatedly thrust the tip of their abdomen into the soil and lay up to fifteen hundred eggs in ten to twenty separate pods. The eggs overwinter in the ground and hatch in the spring as *nymphs*, miniature adults without wings. Throughout the summer, with five to six molts, the nymphs grow to adult size, becoming winged with the final molt. When there is a warm autumn, the egg-laying period is extended and more eggs can be laid. When this is followed by a cool spring and then a dry summer, the grasshopper population swells to its maximum. Cool spring weather delays hatching so that when the young emerge, plants have started to grow and there is a good supply of food. Dry summers slow the growth of fungus that can infect grasshoppers and keep their numbers in check.

Grasshoppers are near the base of the food chain, so when they are plentiful, other prairie wildlife benefits. Dead grasshoppers are consumed by ants, beetles, and crickets. Their eggs are eaten by striped skunks (*Mephitis mephitis*) and long-billed curlews (*Numenius americanus*), and the adults and nymphs are prey for western meadowlarks (*Sturnella neglecta*), American magpies (*Pica hudsonia*), burrowing owls (*Athene cunicularia*), and many other birds. In one study, 85 percent of the food brought to the nests of chestnut-collared longspurs (*Calcarius ornatus*) was prairie hoppers of one species or another.

BIRDS OF THE LEVEL PLAINS
Birds are the most conspicuous residents of the mixed-grass prairie. Roughly 250 species occur in the prairies of Canada and the northern United States. They can be divided into four convenient categories. First, there are the year-round residents, which include such familiar birds as magpies and grouse (Subfamily Tetraoninae). These account for about 15 percent of the total. Seasonal breeders that move to the prairies for the spring and summer are the largest group; roughly half of all prairie birds fall into this category. A third group, the migrants, passes through the prairies in the spring and autumn on the way to and from the boreal forest or the Arctic. This group consists mainly of shorebirds (Order Charadriiformes), waterfowl (Order Anseriformes), and wood warblers (Family Parulidae) and makes up about a quarter of the total. The winter visitors are the smallest group, consisting of just 10 percent of all prairie birds and including such favorites as owls (Family Strigidae), birds of prey (Order Falconiformes), and finches (Family Fringillidae).

The flat, treeless plains are a habitat that presents a special challenge to grassland birds. There are few elevated perches from which to sing and there is little foliage in which to hide their nests. To survive, the birds of the grasslands have evolved fascinating adaptations to deal with both of these challenges.

Male birds sing to inform other males of their presence in a territory and to attract females. Forest birds commonly sing from exposed treetops and elevated branches where they can broadcast their calls and be seen. In contrast, grassland birds, such as Sprague's pipit (*Anthus spragueii*), the chestnut-collared longspur, and the lark bunting (*Calamospiza melanocorys*), make themselves noticeable by singing on the wing, during choreographed aerial flights over their territories. The black-and-white lark bunting rises

No songbird typifies the prairies more than the western meadowlark. Beginning in April, its delightful flutelike song bubbles across the land.

The horned lark is the earliest songbird to nest on the prairies. Its eggs are laid on the ground, often next to a rock or piece of dried cattle dung.

several meters into the air, fixes its wings rigidly above the level of its back, and then gradually floats down in a circle, or an arc, pouring out a series of buzzes and trills. Another noted aerial songster is the high-flying Sprague's pipit. The pipit hangs high in the sky, almost out of sight, sometimes for an hour or so, circling and delivering its thin, metallic jingle.

The absence of trees also affects the nesting behavior of grassland birds, and many of the birds of the level plains, by necessity, build their nests on the ground. The nests of long-billed curlews, killdeers (*Charadrius vociferus*), horned larks (*Eremophila alpestris*), and others are either simple hollow depressions in the ground, with little added material, or small grassy cups, lined with fine feathers and hair, hidden in the grass. The back feathers on all of these birds are heavily patterned in gray and brown to blend with their surroundings, and the eggs of most are blotched and streaked, which protects them when the parents are away from the nest.

Most interesting of all, though, is the acting ability of grassland birds. Many of them have a series of displays meant to distract and lure away predators that approach dangerously close to the nest. Usually, the bird flaps laboriously about the ground, dragging its tail and wings. Soon the predator is in hot pursuit of a seemingly easy victim, but the bird eludes capture by flying off. The fooled animal then moves away in a new direction, typically bypassing the hidden nest.

THE DANCER, THE GYPSY, AND THE TRICKSTER
The behavior of wildlife, particularly that of birds, is the aspect of their lives that fascinates me most. The strategies of courtship and nest selection are intriguing

Two male greater prairie-chickens face off in a territorial boundary squabble. Typically, one or two dozen males gather on a traditional booming ground to strut their stuff.

The marbled godwit, with a wingspan of 80 centimeters (32 in.), is one of the largest prairie shorebirds. It uses its 13-centimeter (5-in.) bill to probe tufts of grass for beetles and grasshoppers.

and a challenge to interpret. The greater sage-grouse (*Centrocercus urophasianus*), brown-headed cowbird (*Molothrus ater*), and burrowing owl are three of my favorites, and their behaviors deserve a closer look.

The greater sage-grouse is the largest grouse in North America. Every year from March to May, the males cluster on traditional dancing grounds, called *leks*, to display and court females. Each male defends a small territory, sometimes less than 15 meters (50 ft.) across. The handsome suitor spreads his tail, struts, and inflates a large, pendulous throat pouch. In the last moments of the display, the air trapped inside the pouch is suddenly released, producing two large pops—the grouse version of a satisfied burp. The center territories of a dancing ground are occupied by the oldest, most dominant males, and for a sex-crazed male, the center of the lek is definitely the place to be. Ninety percent of the hens will mate with the few males displaying in the center of the lek. In fact, in a given year, nine out of ten males never lay a feather on a female. They strut and pop in vain, and like many incurable sports fans, they dream of next season.

The distribution and numbers of sage-grouse have declined dramatically in the last twenty years. Five western states no longer have sage-grouse, and in Canada the population has plummeted by more than 80 percent and now numbers around a thousand birds. The loss of vital sagebrush habitat to cultivation, overgrazing, and burning are the principal culprits.

Originally, the brown-headed cowbird was limited to the open grasslands of the Great Plains. It began to expand beyond the prairies in the early 1800s with the felling of eastern forests, and it now ranges from coast to coast. Formerly, cowbirds were called buffalo birds because of their habit of following bison to feed on insects disturbed by the migrating herds. But this presented a problem. How could the birds keep pace with the movements of the great herds and still feed hungry youngsters back at the nest? The solution for

A dominant male greater sage-grouse displays for a cluster of prospective mates. Ninety percent of hens will mate with dominant males.

the buffalo bird was to become a parasite and lay its eggs in other birds' nests, allowing foster parents to raise its young and freeing itself to follow the shaggy beasts. Typically, the foster parents were smaller birds, such as the yellow warbler (*Dendroica petechia*) or the field sparrow (*Spizella pusilla*), and the alien egg, usually one per nest, "hatched a monster." The buffalo bird nestling, being larger, took most of the food and quickly outgrew its nest mates. Today, we know that a female cowbird may lay forty eggs in a season and successfully parasitize any of 144 species. In many cases, the victims recognize the cowbird egg and either eject it, bury it under the nest lining, or abandon their nest. Even so, the cunning cowbird is successful in up to a third of the nests it parasitizes.

The cowbird survived when the bison did not, but the story of another prairie bird, the burrowing owl (*Athene cunicularia*), is a less successful one. The 25-centimeter-tall (10-in.-tall) burrowing owl, as its name suggests, nests underground. It commonly renovates the abandoned burrows of striped skunks, kangaroo rats (*Dipodomys* spp.), prairie dogs (*Cynomys* spp.), and ground squirrels (*Spermophilus* spp.) for its nest. The owls have the unusual habit of lining the tunnel and nest chamber with dried, shredded cattle or horse manure. A researcher in Oregon speculates that the manure masks the owls' odor and hides their presence from keen-nosed predators such as American badgers (*Taxidea taxus*) and foxes (*Vulpes* spp.). The manure may also attract dung beetles and provide the owls, especially youngsters, with a handy source of food. If you remove the manure, as I once did in a moment of mischievousness, the owls replace it within forty-eight hours.

Burrows are important to the owls, not only as nesting sites, but as refuges from danger. When a golden eagle (*Aquila chrysaetos*) or coyote is sighted, the owls often plunge underground rather than fly away. The diminutive owl protects its burrow in an unusual way. To discourage intruders such as coyotes, weasels

A trio of burrowing owl chicks intently watches for the return of a parent with food. Their diet includes mainly rodents and insects.

(*Mustela* spp.), and bobcats (*Lynx rufus*), cornered adult and young owls mimic the buzzing sound of an angry prairie rattlesnake (*Crotalus viridis viridis*). Since the rattlesnakes also use abandoned burrows as refuges, the owls' sham is a clever one.

Today, the plight of the burrowing owl is sadly similar to that of the northern sage-grouse. Throughout most of its prairie range, the owl has suffered declines, the most drastic being those in Canada where the population may be as low as one thousand pairs. The wholesale war on prairie dogs and ground squirrels, the widespread use of insecticides, and the cultivation and conversion of rangelands to crop lands have all contributed to the declines. The words of the eminent biologist and author Dr. Paul Johnsgard summarize the situation best: "In most western states the familiar 'howdy owl' is saying a long, sad farewell."

LIFE DOWN UNDER

The burrow dwellers of the grasslands are many. They include the burrowing owl, the black-tailed prairie dog (*Cynomys ludovicianus*), Richardson's ground squirrel (*Spermophilus richardsonii*), the badger, the mountain cottontail (*Sylvilagus nuttallii*), Ord's kangaroo rat (*Dipodomys ordii*), and the prairie rattlesnake. Burrows provide all of these animals with a less-severe microclimate and shelter them from the extremes of weather. Seasonal temperature swings are less drastic in burrows. In summer, they are cooler than the open plains, and in winter, they are warmer. Also, the humidity within burrows is higher than aboveground, so that less body moisture is lost to the environment, a vital consideration in the arid prairies.

Among the burrowers, two of the rodents tackle life on the prairies in a completely opposite way. The Richardson's ground squirrel lives in loose, rambling colonies, at times containing several thousand animals. The squirrels follow a surprising pattern of life in which many adult males and females are active for less than four months each year, hibernating for the rest. Adult males are the first to surface in early March. The females emerge about two weeks later and usually mate on their third day out. Baby ground squirrels first appear at the end of May when they are about a month old. By then, many adult males are almost ready to reenter hibernation; the fires of passion are long subdued and their bodies padded with fat. Adult females disappear soon afterward and most are gone by the end of June. From July until September, only the young-of-the-year are active. The early hibernation of adult ground squirrels appears premature. It seems more reasonable that the animals would use as much time as possible to gobble grasses and build up their fat reserves before tackling the energy demands of a lengthy hibernation. However, it seems that the rodents fatten quickly, and as soon as they've added from 20 to 30 percent to their body weight, they're gone. Once the mating season is over and the young are self-sufficient, there is no further reason for the adults to be active aboveground, and hibernation is the surest way to avoid predation from hawks and eagles.

The black-tailed prairie dog, a fellow rodent of the Richardson's ground squirrel, lives life differently. To begin with, prairie dogs do not hibernate, but remain active year round, even during winter on the northern parts of their range. On relatively warm, sunny winter

Adult Richardson's ground squirrels enter hibernation by midsummer, once they have fattened for their long winter fast.

The American badger has long claws to dig out tunneling rodents such as ground squirrels and pocket gophers. The animal hunts mostly at night and spends the day sleeping in its burrow.

days, they may leave their burrows for a short time and move around on the snow. Prairie dogs are also much more gregarious than ground squirrels and live in large colonies, called "dog towns." In former times, some dog towns were beyond imagination. In Texas in the 1800s, there was a prairie dog megalopolis that measured

160 kilometers (100 mi.) by 402 kilometers (250 mi.) and contained an estimated 400 million prairie dogs. Today, the black-tailed prairie dog population is less than 2 percent of what it was in 1900, and the largest dog town is found in the grasslands of northern Mexico where there are a quarter million animals. In Canada, prairie dogs are restricted to a small area along the Frenchman River in southwestern Saskatchewan.

High-density living can have a sinister side, and for black-tailed prairie dogs, the dark family secret is murder. Each year, as many as half of all the newborn pups are killed; the most common killers are adult female relatives. It's unclear what purpose the infanticide serves.

The black-tailed prairie dog and Richardson's ground squirrel share similar adaptations to an underground lifestyle in a flat, treeless habitat. Both squirrels have high-set eyes that facilitate the detection of aerial predators, and both produce alarm calls that alert others in the colony when predators are near. They both have short front legs and long claws for digging, and both have small ears that keep dirt from accumulating.

SNAKE, RATTLE, AND ROLL

The prairie rattlesnake (*Crotalus viridis viridis*) of the Great Plains has the widest distribution of any rattlesnake, ranging from the southern edge of Alberta and Saskatchewan to northern Mexico. It is unique among snakes of the grasslands because it has heat detectors on its face, obviating the need for the serpent to see when it hunts. Just as we can sense the direction of a fireplace from the heat that it throws on our face, a rattlesnake can locate mice, voles, and ground squirrels in complete darkness by detecting the heat these warm-blooded animals emit. Its heat detectors are located in a pair of pits between the eye and nostril. A thin membrane, one-quarter the thickness of this page, stretches across the rear of each pit and is crammed with nerve endings that pick up infrared radiation.

Biologists speculate that rattlesnakes evolved their trademark rattles to alert large grazing animals, such as bison, to their presence, thus avoiding accidental trampling.

The rattlesnake's heat-detecting capacity is extremely sensitive, and the snake can detect temperature differences as subtle as ³⁄₁,₀₀₀ths of a degree.

A rattlesnake's venom glands are at the corners of its jaw and give the snake's head its characteristic triangular shape. The glands are modified salivary glands, which probably evolved initially as aids to digestion and only later acquired their defensive function. The composition of venom is complex—over three dozen separate compounds have been identified. The fangs, which inject the venom, are hinged in the front of the jaw and fold along the roof of the snake's mouth. When the rattlesnake strikes, it throws its head back and the fangs spring down and project forward.

Rattlesnakes in the Canadian prairies, Montana, and the Dakotas are at the northern limit of the species range. The long cold winters and short summers are a challenge for any reptile. In the last twenty years, the miniaturization of radio-telemetry equipment has yielded exciting insights into how these fascinating prairie predators survive. Rattlesnakes that live in these northern areas are active for just five to six months each year, surfacing from their winter dens, called *hibernacula*, in late April and disappearing underground again by early October. Mating occurs in mid to late summer, and the pregnant females give birth the following year, from late summer to early autumn. The cold climate and short warm season greatly affect the snakes. Not only do they grow slower than rattlesnakes that live farther south, but the females breed at an older age and have smaller litters. Northern females usually have their first litter when they are five to seven years old, two or three years later than their southern relatives, and typically they bear just four to a dozen young, versus fifteen to sixteen. As well, because of their limited energy reserves, most northern female rattlesnakes breed only every two or three years instead of yearly. Prairie rattlesnakes, like so many grasslands creatures, demonstrate their adaptability and tenacity to survive.

Every Native American tribe on the plains had its own remedy for rattlesnake bites. Typically, special plants were eaten raw, boiled, or as a broth, or they were applied as a poultice. Usually these measures were combined with the incantations and ministrations of the medicine man. Early cowboys used a hot branding iron to neutralize the poison, or they would pour gun powder over the wound and ignite it. Although this method had a questionable therapeutic effect, it certainly distracted the attention of the victim.

Others used poultices of frogs, toads, and mice. The more repulsive the therapy the greater its presumed merit. In the end, however, the chicken won. Practitioners of the poultry school of snakebite therapy suggested that a whole chicken be split and applied as a poultice, being certain that the head and feathers of the chicken were retained. When the flesh of the chicken turned green or the comb turned blue, the therapy was complete—a foul cure.

THE SAGEBRUSH SPEEDSTER

The one fact that everyone knows about the pronghorn (*Antilocapra americana*) is that it's the fastest mammal in North America. It can sprint at speeds of up to 100 kilometers per hour (60 MPH) and run like this for several kilometers. But this is old news. I knew this bit of nature trivia when I was a child, fifty years ago. Perhaps what is more interesting to consider is *why* the pronghorn is such a speedster. Some of you are already thinking, pronghorns are fast so they can outrun their predators. Well, that could be, but for thousands of years the only large predators on the prairies have been wolves (*Canis lupus*), coyotes (*Canis latrans*), and grizzly bears (*Ursus arctos*). When grizzlies and wolves freely roamed the prairies up until the late 1800s, they may have killed adult pronghorns occasionally, but neither would have regularly preyed on them, as evidenced by the rarity of such events in Yellowstone National Park, where all three animals still live today. What about coyotes then? Well, coyotes do kill pronghorn fawns—in fact, they are the number one predator of fawns—but they virtually never kill an adult. So if pronghorns don't need to outrun their current predators, why are they such speed demons? Researcher and author Dr. John Byers argues that pronghorns are fast, not because of conditions that exist today, but because they are still reacting to the ghosts of predators past, long past.

The pronghorn has been racing over the prairies of North America for nearly 4 million years. Up until just 10,000 years ago, there were many fleet-footed predators hot on its heels. There was the American lion (*Panthera leo atrox*), a larger, faster version of the tawny cat that now rules the plains of Africa, and the predatory American hunting hyena (*Chasmaporthetes ossifragus*), with bone-crushing teeth and the limbs of a cheetah. Also, there was the giant short-faced bear (*Arctodus simus*), which stood as tall as a human's shoulders, ran as fast as a horse, and thrived on meat. But it was two species of cheetahs, the American cheetah (*Acinonyx trumani*) and Studer's cheetah (*A. studeri*), that were most specialized to chase and kill hoofed prey the size of pronghorns, and it seems their memory still haunts the grasslands today. All of these rapacious predators had disappeared by 10,000

A mother swift fox approaches a pair of pups outside their den in southern Alberta. The mother's fur is unkempt because she is midway through her summer molt.

years ago, part of the great wave of extinctions that accompanied humanity's conquest of the continent.

Besides speed, other seemingly unnecessary anti-predator strategies persist in the pronghorns of today. For much of the year, especially in winter, pronghorns live in groups, sometimes numbering in the hundreds. Herding leads to frequent social interactions, which can drain energy with no apparent secondary benefit. Both male and female pronghorns maintain a strict hierarchy, and individuals frequently exercise their rank by intimidating subordinates and displacing them from bedding and feeding areas. Today, the main purpose of these encounters seems to be the simple exercise of power and rank. In the past, however, such a hierarchy would have kept high-ranking individuals in the center of a herd where they were safest from attack. Subordinates would have been relegated to the vulnerable periphery. Also, with dangerous predators no longer prowling the prairies, pronghorns don't need the eyes of neighbors to improve the detection of such danger, nor do they need to hide in the midst of a herd to lessen their chances of being targeted. For me, the idea that animals may retain behaviors for generations beyond their apparent usefulness makes the study of wildlife an exciting detective story, often richer in complexity, intrigue, and surprises than any novel.

HUMANS ON THE PLAINS

The Native Americans of the plains were nomadic hunters and gatherers. Like all cultures based on a similar economy, prairie Native cultures had few possessions and left relatively few artifacts. However, they did leave behind structures of stones that yield some insight into their lives. Scattered throughout the mixed-grass prairie are tepee rings, medicine wheels, and boulder effigies.

Tepee rings were made when Natives placed rocks around the base of their conical tents to anchor them against the perpetual prairie winds. When the people moved their camps, the rocks were left behind as circles of stones, 4 to 5 meters (13 to 16 ft.) in diameter. Although I have found tepee rings on the level plains and in coulees and river bottoms, they are often

found on the edge of escarpments where the former inhabitants could watch for game and enemy tribes.

Medicine wheels were named because of their appearance. At least fifty medicine wheels have been located in the mixed-grass prairies east of the Rockies. The wheels follow a general pattern, usually consisting of a central cairn of rocks with six to twenty-eight spokes radiating out from the center. Often another circle of rocks encloses the spokes. One of the best-known medicine wheels lies atop Medicine Mountain in Wyoming; it is 25 meters (82 ft.) in diameter and contains twenty-eight spokes, with six rock cairns arranged around its rim. A very similar medicine wheel is located on Moose Mountain in southeastern Saskatchewan. The purpose of the wheels is more difficult to explain than their appearance. Perhaps similar wheels were constructed to define the boundaries of a tribe's hunting territory. One popular theory proposes that the spokes of the wheels were designed to align with certain celestial bodies during the summer solstice, the longest day of the year. This was the season of the Sun Dance, celebrated by all prairie tribes, and medicine wheels may have functioned as calendars. Others believe that the wheels were monuments commemorating propitious events or the exploits of a hero. One particular medicine wheel in Alberta is believed to be a memorial to Many Spotted Horses, a Blood war chief. The spokes of the wheel represent his many battle victories.

In winter, pronghorns form large, mixed-sex herds. Dozens of animals may group together. The herds begin to break up in late February and early March.

A mixture of grasses, as well as shrubs including western snowberry, Wood's rose, and silverberry cover the sands in a southern portion of the Great Sand Hills of Saskatchewan.

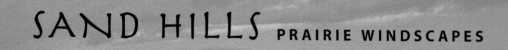

SAND HILLS PRAIRIE WINDSCAPES

AS I STROLLED BACK TO MY CAMP IN THE GREAT SAND HILLS OF SASKATCHEWAN, A PORCUPINE (*ERETHIZON DORSATUM*) SHUFFLED ACROSS THE DUNES. I WAS UPWIND FROM THE ANIMAL, AND IT STOPPED AND FROZE WHEN IT CAUGHT MY SCENT. I MOVED SLOWLY TO ONE SIDE AND IT AMBLED ON, THE QUILLS OF ITS TAIL INSCRIBING ITS SIGNATURE IN THE SAND.

Deer mice are prolific breeders. A female has from two to five litters a year, and each litter commonly contains from four to six young.

It was the end of the day and the sunset held additional promise. The sun stalked the dunes with a fiery eye, and anything that blocked its view was burdened with a lengthy shadow. As the eye reclined, the fire spread and streaked the clouds with crimson. The ebb and flow of color imbued the sky with life, and the clumps of clouds shrank and swelled like the heaving of great lungs. And then it was over, and the molten sky cooled and the porcupine was somewhere in the night. Sand hill areas are the least extensive of the five habitats of the mixed-grass prairie, and some would argue that they are so widely scattered and of such small extent that they do not merit separate consideration. But the unique character of these areas, with their unusual blend of wildlife and plants, warrants a separate chapter.

The mixed-grassland region of each of the Canadian prairie provinces has sand hill areas. In Alberta, there are isolated clusters of long, narrow, grass-covered dunes near Brooks, Taber, and Lethbridge, and north of Medicine Hat, the Middle Sand Hills straddle the South Saskatchewan River. In Manitoba, there are the Lauder Sand Hills, southwest of Brandon, and the Carberry Sand Hills, located in Spruce Woods Provincial Park. In Saskatchewan, there are the Great Sand Hills: 1,900 square kilometers (741 sq. mi.) of sand flats and dunes, located north of the Trans Canada Highway near the Alberta border. In the prairies of the United States, there are sand hill areas in the Bighorn Canyon National Recreation Area that spans the Montana-Wyoming border, in the Pratt Sand Hills Wildlife Area in southwestern Kansas, and in the Great Sand

Dunes National Monument in south-central Colorado. But it is in Nebraska that sand hills rule. North of the Platte River in central Nebraska, a vast tract of sand hills covers 49,980 square kilometers (19,494 sq. mi.), a quarter of the state and the largest area of sand hills in the entire Western Hemisphere. Sadly, my experiences with sand hills are all Canadian, and in the following section I focus primarily on the Great Sand Hills of Saskatchewan. Even so, much of what I cover applies to sand hills throughout the northern prairies.

THE SHAPES OF THE WIND
The Laurentide Ice Sheet began its final withdrawal from the northern prairies 15,000 to 18,000 years ago, ending the Wisconsin Glaciation, which had lasted roughly 100,000 years, and marking the start of the present interglacial period. In the immediate postglacial period the prairies were barren and devoid of vegetation, and the wind had a free hand to work the land. Sands from the shores of old glacial lakes and from outwash plains were assaulted by the wind and shaped into dunes. With time, vegetation returned and stabilized the sand, robbing the wind of its monopoly. Now, Saskatchewan's Great Sand Hills consist of an agglomeration of three identifiable landforms: stabilized dunes covered with grasses and shrubs; active dunes of barren sand; and sand flats, both vegetated and barren. Dunes are always moving, but their level of activity is not constant. Dune movement is greatest during periods of aridity, when drought denudes the sand of vegetation and makes it more vulnerable to the muscle of the wind. The dunes of the Great Sand Hills have moved 1.5 to 4 kilometers (0.9 to 2.5 mi.) since wind erosion started 10,000 years ago, but most of

In most sand hill areas, vegetation has reclaimed the shifting sands and barren dunes cover less than 5 percent of the area.

the dune movement occurred more than 4,000 years ago when there were greater periods of drought.

The three different landforms of the Great Sand Hills—the sand flats, active dunes, and stabilized dunes—produce different microclimates, which, in turn, host different plant communities.

With no vegetation to hold them in place, sand dunes shift and move with the wind. In time, they will likely smother and kill this tree.

Sand flats are either high or low. The sand flats that occupy low-lying regions are generally the most fertile for two reasons: they trap fine, windblown silt and clay particles that enhance the soil by their greater capacity to hold moisture; and, because of runoff from adjacent dunes, there is more water. Here, you will find water-loving willows (*Salix* spp.), trembling aspens (*Populus tremuloides*), and birches (*Betula occidentalis*), with an understory of creeping juniper (*Juniperus horizontalis*) and Wood's rose (*Rosa woodsii*) shrubs. The soil in some low areas accumulates salts, and where this occurs, a saline grassland develops with salt-tolerant species such as silverweed (*Potentilla anserina*), arrow-grass (*Triglochin maritima*), alkali grass (*Puccinella nuttalliana*), and salt grass (*Distichlis stricta*) being the predominant plants. Salty soils are considered again in the chapter on sloughs.

Active dunes are the images that come to mind when most of us think of sand hills. Here, the wind labors over the dunes, brushing the slopes with waves of ripples and drawing the crests into comforting curves. Today, active dunes cover less than 1 percent of the Great Sand Hills. It is a landscape that is shifting and moving under the influence of the predominantly westerly wind. The ripples that form on the surface of the dune, at right angles to the wind, represent the distance that a grain of sand hops ahead when it is lifted by the wind. Presently, the dunes are advancing about 3 meters (9.8 ft.) a year.

The active dunes are a hostile environment for plants and animals. Surface temperatures can rise above 50 degrees Centigrade (122 degrees F.) in summer. Even when it rains, the moisture quickly percolates through the porous sand beyond the reach of most shallow-rooted grasses and shrubs. Nonetheless, over the millennia, plants colonized, conquered, and stabilized the dunes. The earliest grasses to pioneer the dunes are sand dropseed (*Sporobolus cryptandrus*), Indian rice grass (*Oryzopsis hymenoides*), and sand reed grass (*Calamovilfa longifolia*)—all tenacious species with deep roots that reach to the water table. Once these pioneer grasses have secured a foothold and quieted the shifting sands, other grasses and shrubs can move in. But the stabilization of active dunes is a slow, tenuous process. Periods of drought can tip the balance in favor of the dunes and vegetation will die, erasing the results of hundreds of years of growth.

The stabilized dunes are sand dunes that have been subdued by a succession of plants until ground cover is almost complete. This is the most extensive of the three sand hill landscapes and comprises over one half of the area of the Great Sand Hills.

Several microclimates can exist on one stabilized dune if the dune is sufficiently high. North-facing slopes, which have more moisture and are cooler, often support dense growths of western snowberry (*Symphoricarpos occidentalis*), Wood's rose, silverberry (*Elaeagnus commutata*), chokecherry (*Prunus virginiana*), and northern gooseberry (*Ribes oxyacanthoides*). The drier, warmer, south-facing slopes usually support grasslands of Junegrass (*Koeleria cristata*) and needle-and-thread grass or scattered growths of silver sagebrush (*Artemisia frigida*) and creeping juniper.

The variety of environments found within the Great Sand Hills supports a wide array of wildlife in large numbers. Found there is one of the largest populations of sharp-tailed grouse (*Tympanuchus phasianellus*) in Canada and one of the largest populations of mule deer (*Odocoileus hemionus*) in Saskatchewan. Here, there are also Great Plains toads (*Bufo cognatus*), plains spadefoot toads (*Spea bombifrons*), and Ord's kangaroo rats. As well as these, there are at least a hundred other vertebrates and many more beetles, bugs, and spiders.

When a second sharp-tailed grouse settles on a frosted bush, its landing causes a cascade of ice crystals.

THE TIMING OF LIFE

In the evolution of life, those animals that bred when clement weather, food, and shelter were available had a greater survival of offspring than those that bred at less-propitious times. Thus, natural selection favored those animals that could time their breeding cycles best. Wild animals use a number of environmental cues as timing devices: tidal cycles, rainfall cycles, temperatures, and the seasonal changes in day length. In the temperate to northern latitudes, day length is the most reliable and consistent cue. For example, in March, the increasing day length is perceived by the brain of the sharp-tailed grouse, urging it to dance when all else is quiet. Under this stimulus, the brain of the grouse produces a hormone that stimulates the recrudescence of the bird's testes or ovaries.

In the Great Sand Hills of Saskatchewan, late March is an empty time. The landscape is leached of color, and the bite of winter lingers as deer and pronghorn move slowly, rationing their strength. Silence pervades, the insects are locked in hibernation, and the songbirds are still a month away. The ground is frozen and brittle underfoot, the plants firmly held in check. But, out on a grassy knoll, life refuses to be restrained, and the sharp-tails dance. Each spring, the sharp-tailed grouse assemble on ancestral dancing grounds, as do sage-grouse and prairie-chickens (*Tympanuchus* spp.), to reenact their courtship rituals. The males coo, cluck, and strut. With their heads down and their tails pointed to the sky, they rapidly stomp their feet, and little clouds of dust erupt around them. The birds vibrate across the ground like wound-up toys; they run feverishly for a moment and then suddenly stop. Up to forty males may gather on a dancing ground, called a *lek,* half the size of a football field. Each male defends his own small patch of prairie. One by one, female grouse wander through the cluster of males, assessing the dancers for qualities only they can detect, looking for a mate. Once the hen makes her choice, she mates just once and then leaves.

The day length, or *photoperiod*, not only coordinates the breeding cycle of the sharp-tailed grouse, but also synchronizes many other aspects of animal behavior and governs the lives of many grassland mammals, birds, and insects. The photoperiod synchronizes the arrival and departure of migrating birds and the establishment of avian territories. It times the seasonal changes in coat color (from brown to white and back again) of weasels (*Mustela* spp.) and white-tailed jackrabbits (*Lepus townsendii*) and stimulates the growth of thick winter fur in coyotes and badgers. As well, the photoperiod drives ground squirrels into hibernation, and it arrests the development of insects in a phase preparatory for winter and then stimulates their emergence in spring.

The changes in photoperiod are also the primary regulators of antler growth in deer. The increasing photoperiod in spring stimulates the pituitary gland in the brain of the male mule deer, and the hormones produced initiate antler growth in April and May. The growing antlers are covered with "velvet," a fur-covered skin that carries nerves and blood vessels to the growing antler. Somewhat later, different hormones from the pituitary gland, also under the influence of day length, stimulate growth of the buck's testes. As the rut approaches in the fall, male sex hormones

The mule deer rut occurs in late October and November. Mature bucks may fight violently with each other and risk injury, even death, for the right to breed.

A white-tailed jackrabbit stretches as it leaves its daytime resting site, a shallow depression in the snow. These hares are primarily active at night.

from the enlarging testes block the action of pituitary antler-growth hormones, the antlers stop growing, and the velvet dries up. At this time the bucks thrash their antlers against bushes and trees, and as the velvet is rubbed off, the antlers become polished and stained brown with resin. Finally, as the photoperiod shortens in late autumn and early winter, the pituitary gland is no longer stimulated, and this leads to a reduction in the stimulation of the testes. As a result, the level of male sex hormones decreases. This causes the connection between the deer's skull and its antlers to lose calcium and weaken, and the antlers eventually fall off. The return of longer days in the spring starts the cycle again.

ORD'S KANGAROO RATS

The jovial woman in the small prairie café asked me why I was in town. When I told her I wanted to see an Ord's kangaroo rat, she was incredulous. "You drove 300 kilometers (185 mi.) to see a rat?" She laughed so hard I thought she would drop the coffee pot she was holding. "You city folks sure know how to have fun." Later that night, under a clear, moonless prairie sky, I scooped up one of the small, long-tailed rodents and examined it closely as it sat placidly in the palm of my hand, its silvery whiskers twitching. I had fun, lots of fun.

In Canada, Ord's kangaroo rat (*Dipodomys ordii*) is classified as a vulnerable species and is restricted to a few sand hill areas in southeastern Alberta and southwestern Saskatchewan. Even so, of the seventeen species of kangaroo rats found in North America, Ord's is the most common and widespread, ranging along the entire length of the mixed-grass prairies from southern Canada to central Mexico.

Kangaroo rats are primarily rodents of the desert, and the greatest variety of species live in the American southwest. Not surprisingly, all kangaroo rats, including Ord's of the grasslands, are well adapted to conserve moisture. Kangaroo rats are loners, each

Arctic-nesting snowy owls often migrate to the northern prairies in winter where they hunt jackrabbits, cottontails, grouse, pheasants, and waterfowl.

defending an extensive network of tunnels where it spends the daylight hours. Typically, underground tunnels are relatively cool and high in humidity, so when the rodents breathe they lose less moisture through their lungs than if they were active aboveground during the heat of the day. Besides losing moisture through their lungs, all mammals lose moisture in their urine and feces. Kangaroo rats minimize these losses by producing powder-dry droppings and urine that is extremely concentrated—four times more concentrated than that of the most parched of humans. Mother kangaroo rats have the added strain of nursing and compensate for this by producing the most concentrated milk of any land mammal we know. The rodents' underground tunnels provide a final advantage in their struggle to conserve moisture. K-rats are seedeaters, and they store surplus seeds in underground caches. The dry seeds absorb moisture from the humid air of the tunnels and their water content may actually triple.

Kangaroo rats are on the menu of many animals, so it's no surprise that their behavior is greatly influenced by the threat from talons and teeth. The rodents get their common name from the way they hop about on their muscular rear legs. Bipedal locomotion gives them speed and maneuverability, and their long tail acts as a counterweight. All kangaroo rats are strictly nocturnal—another tactic to conserve moisture—but the threat of predators modifies their nighttime behavior. At least five species of owls, as well as coyotes, foxes, weasels, bobcats, and badgers, hunt at night, so kangaroo rats avoid moonlit nights or switch to areas of their territory where there is protective shrubbery to give them cover. Snakes, especially rattlesnakes (*Crotalus*

The large rear legs and feet of the Ord's kangaroo rat enable it to hop about rapidly on two legs. It uses its long tail for balance and maneuverability.

After a thunderstorm, a juvenile Swainson's hawk spreads its wings to dry off in the sunshine.

spp.), also hunt at night, and the closely related banner-tailed kangaroo rat (*Dipodomys spectabilis*) has a novel way to discourage them. It kicks dirt in their face and stomps its feet in a threatening way, behaviors that may also be used by Ord's kangaroo rat. All snakes are deaf to airborne sounds, but they readily detect ground vibrations transmitted through the bones of their lower jaw. Researchers speculate that when a kangaroo rat "footdrums," it's telling the snake it has been seen, and the snake leaves to search for a less-suspecting victim. It's this surprising variety of animal strategies that has kept me fascinated with the natural world for over forty years. I'm happy to be a critter junkie.

GNOMES OF THE NIGHT

Toads are usually associated with moist conditions, yet two seldom-seen species, the Great Plains toad and the plains spadefoot toad, are found throughout the semi-arid grasslands. It seems paradoxical because the greatest problem that toads and all amphibians face is dehydration, but within many prairie areas there are roadside ditches, flooded fields, farm dugouts, small streams, and ephemeral sloughs that allow them to survive.

Toads breathe through their lungs and their skin. In winter, they bury themselves in mud, and at this time, cutaneous respiration becomes more important than pulmonary respiration. To be an effective respiratory organ, skin must be moist and permeable and have a rich blood supply, but these same characteristics make the animals vulnerable to dehydration since moisture readily evaporates from their skin. To lessen the danger from dehydration, prairie toads are active at night when humidity is relatively high and temperatures cool. If conditions are too dry, the plains spadefoot toad may stay buried in the soil for months at a time. Spadefoots are named for the stiff tubercle on each of their rear legs that helps them to dig backward to depths of almost a meter (3 ft.).

These plains spadefoot toads are locked in the amphibian version of a sexual embrace, called amplexus. The male will cling to the female until she is finished laying her eggs.

Toads are active at night for a second reason: it's safer. Lacking teeth or claws, toads are defenceless and rely on nocturnal activity, secretive behavior, cryptic coloration, and distasteful skin secretions to protect them from predators. The skin of most toads contains poison glands, which are especially abundant in the almond-shaped parotoid glands behind the animals' eyes. The parotoid glands produce a milky, viscous secretion that, in North American species, is not dangerous to humans. (The skin secretions of some poison-dart frogs [Family Dendrobatidae] that live in the Neotropics of Central and South America are lethal to humans and among some of the most deadly of toxins.) When a prairie toad is grabbed by a predator, the noxious skin secretions may cause inflammation and burning in the predator's mouth and throat or even nausea. Often, the toad is released immediately and hops away unharmed. Furthermore, the distasteful experience may dissuade the predator from ever tackling a toad in the future. Severe reactions such as convulsions, muscle paralysis, and cardiac arrest that often afflict predators that attempt to eat poison-dart frogs never occur with attacks on prairie toads.

One grassland predator, the western hognose snake (*Heterdon nascius*), has a special taste for toads and appears immune to their skin secretions. When a hognose first approaches a toad, the toad rises high on its legs and gulps air, inflating its body in an attempt to intimidate and discourage its attacker. The hognose is generally not impressed by the bluff and promptly grabs the puffy toad and starts to swallow it. Hognose snakes appear to have evolved a number of adaptations for a diet of toads, called *bufophagy*. First, they have a wide gape and highly mobile upper jaw, which helps them engulf oversized prey. Enlarged teeth at the rear of their upper jaw inject a mild venom and at the same time puncture the toad, deflating its body, not to mention its self-confidence, and making it easier to swallow. Finally, the hognose seems especially resistant to toad

The upturned scale on the end of the nose of the western hognose snake helps it to dig in sand and loose soil.

venom, possibly because of the snake's large adrenal glands which are believed to detoxify the poison.

Although toads are preyed upon by many animals, they are predators themselves, capturing beetles, ants, moths, and spiders with their long, sticky tongues. Of the numerous spiders known today, many of them were first described from partially digested specimens taken from the stomachs of toads. The spiders of the sand hill areas of the prairies far outnumber the toads, and theirs is the next story I want to tell.

WOLVES WITH EIGHT LEGS

Spiders (Class Arachnida) are among the oldest terrestrial animals, dating back to the Carboniferous Period, 300 million years ago. Many people mistakenly think of them as insects (Class Insecta), which are an entirely different group of invertebrates. Insects have three body segments (head, thorax, and abdomen), three pairs of legs attached to their thorax, and a pair of antennae sprouting from the top of their head. Spiders, on the other hand, have no antennae, only two body segments (a combined head and thorax, called a *cephalothorax*, and an abdomen), and four pairs of legs. Spiders are also distinctive in their feeding habits, their use of fangs and venom to subdue prey, and the many uses they have for silk.

Spiders have evolved into two broad categories: active hunters that chase and subdue prey and web builders that ensnare it. The grasses of the prairies provide very poor anchorage for flimsy, silken webs, so web-building spiders are relatively uncommon in the grasslands. In contrast, hunting spiders are very common, and among these, the wolf spiders (Family Lycosidae) are the most numerous. Most spiders have eight eyes, arranged in two rows of four each. The eyes of web-building spiders are small and relatively weak because they rely on vibrations transmitted through the silk strands of their web to alert them to the presence of prey. Wolf spiders have no web and locate prey solely by vision. They also have eight eyes, but two of them are greatly enlarged for greater visual acuity. Their large eyes are readily visible with the human eye.

The scientific name for the wolf spider family comes from the Greek word *lycosa*, which means "to tear like a wolf." These spiders are quick and fearless. They run and pounce on their prey, then inject it with venom through long, pointed fangs. A wolf spider's prey may be bigger than it is and is often covered with a hard exoskeleton that is not easily torn apart. To solve this problem, wolf spiders flood their prey with digestive juices from their mouth that transform the inside of the prey into a liquefied broth, which is then sucked up.

Female wolf spiders may behave like a pit-bull terrier when hunting, but when it comes to mothering, they are some of the most caring creatures. Most female spiders hide their silken egg sac in some secluded nook and then forget about it. The mother wolf spider attaches the egg sac to the tip of her abdomen and carries it around with her at all times. When the young are finally ready to hatch, the mother carefully tears open the silken sac, releasing the spiderlings. They pour out and climb onto her back, where special club-shaped bristles help the young to hold on. There may be more than a hundred spiderlings resting on top of each other in several layers. The young spiders ride on their mother's back until they are about a week old and have molted for the first time. During this week, the mother wolf spider continues to run, hunt, and burrow, and the spiderlings must hold on or perish. When they finally leave the security of their mother, the young spiders climb to the top of nearby vegetation and face into the wind. They secrete a long thread of silk from the tip of their abdomen, which is caught by the wind and wafts them aloft on a gossamer kite. This behavior, called *ballooning*, may carry a spiderling a few dozen meters or hundreds of kilometers, enabling the species to colonize distant grasslands.

THE MOUND MAKER

Common within the prairies are small mounds of earth that seem to lack a maker. There are no animals running about, and no holes can be seen. The mounds frequently occur in groups and may form a straight line; sometimes they are linked together by a rope of elevated earth. The mounds are often mistakenly attributed to moles (Family Talpidae), but there are no moles in the grasslands. The mysterious mounds are the work of the secretive northern pocket gopher (*Thomomys talpoides*). The pocket gopher should not be confused with the ground squirrels (*Spermophilus* spp.) that some people call gophers. Although both the ground squirrels and the pocket gophers are rodents that live in burrows, ground squirrels spend much of their time aboveground and are frequently seen, whereas pocket gophers rarely leave their burrows and are practically never seen.

The northern pocket gopher is a little smaller than an average ground squirrel and is all teeth and claws—the consummate tunneler. To offset the continual wear on the tools of its trade, the front claws of a pocket gopher grow 14 centimeters (5.5 in.) a year, and its chisel-shaped lower incisors grow a remarkable 43 centimeters (17 in.). The animal's lips close behind its teeth so that it can excavate soil without getting dirt in its mouth.

The skin of the pocket gopher is loose, allowing the animal to move about easily in the confinement of its burrow, and its fur is short and silky so that soil doesn't adhere to it. Common to many fossorial mammals, the pocket gopher has small eyes and tiny, external ears. In the muffled, lightless world of its underground maze, sight and hearing are less important to the pocket gopher than a sense of smell and touch. The gopher has many sensitive bristles on its face and wrists, which help it stay in touch with its tunnels. It even has sensitive bristles on the tip of its tail, a helpful feature when it crawls backward, something it often does.

The pocket gopher derives its name from a pair of external, fur-lined cheek pouches that open at the sides of its mouth and extend along either side of its neck. The "pockets," which can be turned inside out like pant pockets, are used to carry food and bedding material.

The earthworks of the pocket gopher are the most conspicuous sign of its presence. As it searches for food, the animal digs an extensive network of subterranean tunnels. It eats mainly roots and tubers and sometimes pulls an entire plant down through the surface soil into its burrow. The characteristic mounds are formed when the animal tunnels to the surface and pushes up the surplus soil. During a five-month study, one pocket gopher dug 146 meters (480 ft.) of tunnels and piled up 161 mounds, sometimes 14 in a single day.

The researcher estimated the rodent might move 1,130 kilograms (2,490 lb.) of soil in a year.

Many grassland mammals excavate and live in burrows, but the pocket gopher is the only one that plugs the entrance to its burrow with soil so that it is largely cut off from the outside air. Thus, the animal creates a closed environment, with both benefits and hazards. In a closed system of tunnels, the humidity is high, 85 to 95 percent, and the gopher can maintain its water balance just with the moisture in its food. In a closed system, however, the level of oxygen may be quite low, and the buildup of carbon dioxide, which the animal exhales in normal respiration, may be very high. Concentrations of carbon dioxide as high as sixty times that of atmospheric air have been recorded. The pocket gopher can deal with low concentrations of oxygen because of its slow rate of metabolism, but it is still unclear how the animal endures such high levels of carbon dioxide, normally considered lethal.

The northern pocket gopher is found throughout the mixed grasslands, especially in regions where the soil is loose and easy to excavate. In agricultural areas, the pocket gopher is viewed as a pest, particularly where alfalfa is grown, since it not only consumes the plant but its mounds also make it more difficult to harvest the crop. To farmers and home gardeners, the animal can cause considerable damage and economic loss. But before humans arrived on the prairies, the pocket gopher was a valuable part of the ecosystem. One researcher opined: "The constant digging action counteracts the packing effect of grazers, such as cattle and bison, and makes the soil more porous, slowing spring run-off as well as providing more aeration for plant roots." Perhaps the pocket gopher deserves our admiration more than our disdain.

The front teeth of the northern pocket gopher grow continually to offset wear. Its chisel-shaped incisors may grow a remarkable 44 centimeters (17 in.) in a year!

In winter, the porcupine feeds almost exclusively on the bark of trees and woody shrubs. In summer, it shifts from the treetops to the ground where it nibbles on green leafy vegetation.

Native Americans
called autumn the
"geese going days"
when the skies
filled with honking
waterfowl and the
coulees blazed with
color.

COULEES VALLEYS OF DISCOVERY

AUTUMN IS MY FAVORITE SEASON. COOL DAYS, WANING DAYLIGHT, AND GEESE OVERHEAD CREATE AN AIR OF GENTLE MELANCHOLY AS THE GREENS OF SUMMER ARE TOUCHED WITH SCARLET, GOLD, AND ORANGE. I REMEMBER MOST VIVIDLY AN OCTOBER DAY WHEN I EXPLORED A COULEE NEAR EASTEND, SASKATCHEWAN. IT WAS BITTERLY COLD, AND A STRONG WIND MUSCLED ITS WAY OUT OF THE NORTHWEST, NUMBING MY CHEEKS, BUT I FELT ABLAZE WITH LIFE.

Aspens encrusted
with hoarfrost
sparkle in the winter
cold of a prairie
dawn.

The land was in full conversation with the wind, and the whisper of leaves and chatter of branches were often interrupted by the cries and groans of bending trunks. The air was rich and heavy with fragrance, and I inhaled deeply to taste it with my lungs. As I strolled, I chewed on a blade of grass as I often do when I feel content. Just when I thought that things could not be better, I looked overhead and a prairie falcon (*Falco mexicanus*) sliced across the sky. The bird was untamed, unfettered, and vital. I felt the same.

If it can be said that there are forests within the grasslands, then these forests are found in coulees—the wooded valleys and ravines of the prairies, often embracing the banks of rivers and creeks. Within a coulee there is a great variety of vegetation, determined by the depth of the valley, the steepness of the slope, the direction of the slope, and most of all by the amount of moisture in the soil. I think of coulees as the only grassland habitat that sometimes has a roof. Because the vegetation has height, the habitat can be viewed as three separate levels, although the levels are not always distinct and some may be absent.

The top level of a forested coulee is the canopy, formed by the crowns of trees like trembling aspen (*Populus tremuloides*), plains cottonwood (*Populus deltoides*), green ash (*Fraxinus pennsylvanica*), and Manitoba maple (*Acer negundo*). The second level is comprised of young trees and bushy shrubs like snowberry, silver buffaloberry (*Shepherdia argentea*), and shrubby cinquefoil (*Potentilla fruticosa*). On the ground level are the grasses and wildflowers. Each level receives a different combination of sunlight, moisture, wind, and temperature, which yields a different microclimate. The canopy is the harshest of the three levels, receiving the full force of the wind and rain and the full impact of the sun's heating rays. Lower down, conditions are less extreme, and on the ground, there is little wind and more constant temperatures and humidity.

The stratification of vegetation in a forested coulee allows a greater variety of wildlife to live in the habitat. Some creatures are associated with only a single vegetation level, whereas others may range over all three. For example, deer mice (*Peromyscus maniculatus*), ground squirrels, and shrews (*Sorex* spp.) use the lowest level, while deer and porcupines feed on the shrubs and saplings. Birds are the most mobile of the wildlife of the coulee and may use all three levels, but often show a preference for one or two. As ruffed grouse (*Bonasa umbellus*), brown thrashers (*Toxostoma rufum*), and spotted towhees (*Pipilo maculatus*) scratch and forage at ground level, woodpeckers (*Picoides* spp.), nuthatches (*Sitta* spp.), and brown creepers (*Certhis americana*) work the trunks of trees, vireos (*Vireo* spp.) and wood warblers (Family Parulidae) scour the leaves of the canopy for spiders and insects, and Swainson's hawks (*Buteo swainsoni*) scream at intruders from the tops of the tallest trees. But the greatest variety and numbers of prairie animals are not found in any of these forest levels, but within the soil. Here, there exists a miniature ecosystem with its own guild of herbivores, carnivores, and scavengers.

LIFE IN THE SOIL

Within the soil of the coulee, dead leaves and old roots and stems decompose slowly. The process may start with an earthworm (*Lumbricus terrestris*) ingesting some of the dead vegetation. The worm's excrement will contain some of the nutrients it ingested, as well as bacteria added from its own intestinal tract. This excrement, in turn, is ingested by other soil animals, which absorb some more of the lingering nutrients and then add their own bacterial flora to what remains. Along the way, fungi (Kingdom Mycota) and protozoans (Kingdom Protozoa) may also become involved in the chain of decomposition. After multiple ingestions, the organic matter is eventually broken down into simple chemical compounds, which can then be reabsorbed by plants and used for their own growth and reproduction. When the plants die, the material is returned to the soil to start the cycle again. If the cycle is interrupted at any step, the soil may deteriorate. This occurs in agriculture when crops are removed from the cycle, and the nutrients must be replaced by synthetic fertilizers.

Soil animals are essential for the recycling of nutrients in the coulee. They form a complex community of predators and prey, intricately adapted to their environment. All of these microscopic animals rely on a highly developed sense of smell and touch. Tactile hairs cover their bodies and inform them about their world. Many of the animals that live in the deeper layers of the soil are blind. Nevertheless, they still sense light, and if exposed to it for even a brief time, they become restless and move about until they find a dark refuge in which to hide. Most soil creatures also exhibit *thigmotropism*—the desire to be touched on all sides—which manifests itself in a tendency to crawl into narrow cracks and gaps in the earth.

Male robins return to the prairies in early April, several weeks before the females do. Arriving so early, they may have to endure the challenge of a late spring snowstorm.

In autumn, the diminishing hours of daylight and cool temperatures allow colorful pigments within the leaves to show through.

Many soil animals, especially beetle mites (Order Oribatida) and springtails (Order Collembola), feed on the roots of decaying plants. These animals are preyed upon by roundworms (Phylum Nematoda). In turn, various fungi prey on the roundworms, and some of the fungi are ingenious trappers. One type of fungus trap consists of a network of highly adhesive hoops that entangles the worm. Once a worm is tethered, a fine filament of the fungus penetrates the animal's body, then fills it and absorbs the contents, leaving only the animal's skin. Another fungus trap operates like an animal snare. The fungus has ring filaments attached to the main filament. When a roundworm passes through one of the rings, the friction of its body stimulates the ring cells to swell and grip the worm. The ring expansion is exceptionally rapid, one-tenth of a second, and the worm has little chance of survival.

Animals that live in the soil have the same requirements as animals aboveground: space, oxygen, water, and food. The soil environment offers protection from desiccating winds, lethal ultraviolet rays, and extremes of temperature, but if the soil becomes saturated with water, the air within the cracks and spaces of the soil is displaced and the animals may drown. If the soil dries out or freezes, the tiny creatures must either penetrate deeper or enclose themselves in a cyst or capsule and await better conditions.

TICK TALK

In my years of medical practice in the emergency department in Regina, I saw ticks, and I saw people, and they always came together. Ticks (Order Acarina) are parasites that attach themselves to the skin of wild animals and humans to feed on their blood. Only a tick's mouthparts penetrate the skin, so the offending creature can easily be pulled loose by grasping it with a pair of tweezers. In the past, some time-honored remedies for removal included dousing the objectionable beast with alcohol or gasoline or branding it with a hot needle. Researchers now caution that such tactics may "annoy" the tick, causing it to regurgitate fluids that could be potentially infective.

In the northern grasslands there are two common species of ticks that target the hot-blooded bodies of humans: the dog tick (*Dermacentor variabilis*) and the Rocky Mountain wood tick (*D. andersoni*). The dog tick is found in brushy areas, poplar groves, and riversides in the eastern half of the grasslands from southeastern Saskatchewan and the Dakotas eastward. The wood tick occurs in the western grasslands and prefers coulees and shrub-covered hillsides, especially where saskatoon and rose bushes grow and where there are jackrabbits and ground squirrels.

Ticks are related to spiders, scorpions, and mites and resemble tiny watermelon seeds with eight legs. They have three stages in their life cycle, and at each stage, blood is taken from a different victim; frequently, the hosts are three different species of animals. In a typical life cycle, the newly hatched larva, called a *seed tick*, feeds on a deer mouse (*Peromyscus maniculatus*), a meadow vole (*Microtus pennsylvanicus*), or a least chipmunk (*Tamias minimus*); the intermediate stage, called a *nymph*, feeds on a ground squirrel, porcupine, or jackrabbit; and the adult stage feeds on a coyote, a deer, or a human. Ticks are tough critters. Any of the stages can overwinter in the grass and survive for a year or more without a meal. Adults may even survive as long as two or three years.

The adult ticks, the usual ones to feed on humans, are most active in the spring, and they persist until the end of June. They climb to the top of a blade of grass along a game trail and wait for a passing animal.

The fleshy appendage above the beak of the male wild turkey is called a snood. In dominant males, the snood lengthens and flushes with color. These rival males illustrate this well.

Vibrations, carbon dioxide, or shadows get them excited. They frantically wave their legs, called *questing*, hoping to grab a hot-blooded donor. Specially adapted hooks on the ticks' forelegs help them cling to their victim. Ticks don't jump or drop from the trees; that kind of coordination takes more brain power than they have. Ticks are very sensitive to gravity, called *negative geotropism*, and as soon as they attach to a host, they climb upward, often settling on the animal's head or shoulders. Within a few hours, they attach themselves with their mouthparts. Their salivary glands produce a whitish, cement-like substance around the bite that prevents them from being easily detached. They also produce an anesthetic that makes their bite painless so their presence is unsuspected.

Both male and female ticks drink blood, but their blood-sucking behavior differs. Typically, males feed intermittently, but do not take much blood, and spend most of their time crawling around the host looking for partners. The females stay attached to one spot, where they may spend up to seven days engorging themselves. They need blood to produce eggs and may swell to a revolting length of 1.5 centimeters (0.6 in.), increasing their original weight by more than a hundred fold. In human terms, this would be equivalent to an average woman sitting down and eating continuously until she weighed 5 metric tons.

The roving males, not surprisingly, have a single thought in mind: sex. That's right, ticks first take your blood, then they mate on you. After mating, the engorged females drop from the host and soon lay 5,000 to 10,000 small, brown eggs, usually in one large mass, under a rock or some dried grass. The females die soon afterward, and the eggs usually hatch the following spring as seed ticks, starting the cycle anew.

Ticks can transmit a number of human illnesses, including Rocky Mountain spotted fever, tick paralysis, and Lyme disease. But all of these ailments are rare and curable. The fear of ticks should never deter anyone from reaping the rewards of a spring stroll through a prairie coulee. If you're not comforted by these words, may I suggest you follow the advice of one researcher who suggested "wrapping your body in plastic and hiding under your bed to reduce your chances of picking up a tick."

ABUNDANCE TO BONES: THE STORY OF THE BISON

In the northern prairies, the mixed grasslands were the summer range of the bison. In autumn, most of the animals migrated north and west out of the grasslands to spend the winter in the foothills and the aspen parkland. The bison were the center of life for prairie Native Americans, who followed the herds wherever they moved. The people hunted the animals in a number of ways. They stalked them on their hands and knees, or they herded them into deep snow where the mired animals were easy to overtake. They also built corrals at the end of steep-sided coulees and drove the bison into them. The most successful hunting technique was the buffalo jump, a steep cliff over which the big, shaggy beasts were driven to their death. Days before a drive, the young men of the tribe would locate the bison and move the herd slowly toward the jump site, using smoke from smouldering dung. Frequently, stone cairns were built in the configuration of a funnel that led to the cliff. When the young men had the bison close enough, the animals were stampeded into the funnel. Other people hid behind the cairns and jumped up, waving and shouting to heighten the panic of the fleeing animals.

In the northern prairies, Montana was the center of this hunting technique; it has 245 buffalo jumps, while Alberta has 60, Saskatchewan 20, and North and South Dakota, Wyoming, and Manitoba have one each. The most famous buffalo jump is Head-Smashed-In, located on the edge of the Porcupine Hills in southern Alberta. In 1981, the United Nations Educational, Scientific, and Cultural Organization (UNESCO) designated the area as a World Heritage Site in recognition of its important cultural significance. Head-Smashed-In was used as a kill site by Aboriginal peoples for 5,500 years.

All of the buffalo jumps face east and north, a reflection of the geomorphology, the prevailing winds, and the bison's acute sense of smell. The remains at buffalo jumps show a predominance of cows over bulls. Because female bison show a greater wariness and willingness to run, this may have made them more susceptible and preferable for driving.

Both the corral and the buffalo jump were dependent upon topographical features. The introduction of the horse enabled the indigenous people to hunt bison anywhere, anytime, and by the mid-1700s, all the tribes on the northern plains were mounted. By 1780, bison hunting had become commercialized, with Native hunters supplying hides and pemmican (dried bison meat mixed with fat and berries) to the fur-trading posts in the north.

The bison were eliminated first from the southern prairies. By 1830, meat and hide hunters were looking to the northern prairies to continue their livelihood. The northern bison herd is estimated to have contained 5 million animals, but was decimated in less than three decades. After the hunters left, the bone pickers came. Bison bones were sold for six to ten dollars per ton. The bones were ground up and used in refining sugar. Horns were fashioned into buttons, combs, and knife handles. The bone trade was over by the 1890s, and the herds were gone forever.

We may take some consolation from recent paleoclimatology studies. We now know that the average annual rainfall on the prairies decreased in the late 1800s. This produced a deterioration of the grasslands and a reduced capacity of the prairie to support large numbers of grazing animals. If the bison had not already been eliminated, the grasslands would have been overstocked, and it's probable that three-quarters of the buffalo population would have disappeared with no help from greedy humans.

SILENTLY, IN THE NIGHT

So much of our lives are bathed in artificial light that few of us ever experience the delights of darkness. The healthy human eye takes roughly thirty to forty minutes to become maximally adjusted to the dark, after which its sensitivity increases 10,000 fold. Surprisingly, some humans, given the necessary time to adapt to darkness, can see as well at night as many species of owls. I've often wandered in nature at night, and nothing awakens the mind and sends my blood rushing like a walk in a prairie coulee after the sun goes down.

Because darkness is such an alien environment for humans, it has always been a time of mystery, and

A THOUSAND CAUTIOUS EYES DO SCAN, EACH SHADOW AND EACH FORM;

AWARE ARE ALL, THIS NIGHT THERE TREADS A STRANGER TO THIS PLACE.

THE STRANGER MOVES AS ONE WHO FEARS DESPITE ITS SIZE AND BULK,

AND CLAMMY SKIN THAT SHINES WITH SWEAT BETRAYS AN INNER STRESS.

WITH STEPS UNSURE AND BRAIN CONFUSED IT SLOWLY WENDS ITS WAY,

EACH SOUND IS GRASPED WITH HUNGRY EARS, EACH SMELL INHALED WITH ZEST.

ITS EYES REACH OUT LIKE GROPING HANDS FOR SHAPES IT CANNOT SEE,

AND IN ITS HEAD THE CIRCUITS RACE TO SOLVE THE SHADOWED WORLD.

IN FORMER TIMES IT ROAMED THIS LAND, AND FELT AKIN TO ALL,

BUT NOW IT DWELLS WHERE EVERY STEP IS MARKED BY GLARING LIGHTS;

BUT FOR A TIME THE STRANGER DARED, AS MAN RETURNED TO NIGHT.

— WAYNE LYNCH

we are fascinated by creatures that can operate under such challenging circumstances. No creature embodies "the dead of the night" more than does the owl. Two nocturnally active species of owls, the great horned owl (*Bubo virginianus*) and the long-eared owl (*Asio otus*), nest in coulees in many areas of the northern prairies. British researcher Dr. Graham Martin notes that an owl's ability to fly and hunt in darkness is not the result of a single sense, a magical sixth sense, but the combined effort of two normal senses, sight and hearing, working together.

Everybody knows owls are denizens of the night, or are they? Worldwide, there are over two hundred species of owls, yet maybe as few as 30 percent of them are strictly nocturnal. Studies done in the 1950s and 1960s claimed that the night vision in owls was as much as three hundred times greater than in humans. These extravagant claims are still quoted today. There's just one problem—they are wrong. The studies done fifty years ago were flawed, and more recent research suggests that, at best, the night vision of owls is only two to three times better than ours. Even so, how do they do it?

To begin with, owls have large eyes. Those of a great horned owl are the largest of any owl in North America and as big as an adult human's. Large eyes can project a large image on the retina at the rear of the eye, and a large image carries more information than a small one. More important, however, is the superior light-gathering ability of an owl's eye, which is controlled by the size of the bird's pupils. A large pupil admits a large amount of light. In the jargon of photography, the human eyeball has an f/stop of 2.1, whereas that of some nocturnal owls is 1.3. When comparing f/stops, the smaller the number, the larger the pupil size; thus, the eyes of some owls can admit 2.7 times more light than can the eyes of a human. Another feature that allows owls to fly about at night is the speed with which they can focus their eyes, which is ten times faster than humans. This enables them to see obstacles quickly and to make flight adjustments to avoid dangerous collisions.

A well-developed sense of hearing is the second asset displayed by long-eared and great horned owls, as well as by many other nocturnal owls. Most birds have small, round ear openings, whereas many owls have large, half-moon-shaped vertical ear slits. The slits on either side often differ in size and position, with one side usually being larger and higher on the head. Because of the asymmetry in the ear openings, a sound is perceived by one ear fractionally sooner than the other; the time difference may be as little as 3/100,000ths of a second. As well, the sound will be louder in the ear nearest to the source. This sensitivity allows an owl to pinpoint the location of a sound with remarkable accuracy. The feathery ear tufts that are the source of the common names of the long-eared owl and the great horned owl are used solely for display and camouflage and have nothing to do with hearing.

Noisy wings mask faint sounds and could interfere with an owl's detection of prey when the bird is flying and hunting. To minimize such background noise, owl flight is especially quiet, so the birds can use their ears to best advantage. Because the wings on many owls are large for their body weight, the noise from flapping is minimal. As well, the feathers on the leading and trailing edges of the birds' wings are fringed.

This reduces turbulence, another potential source of distracting noise.

Having touted the hearing ability of owls, it turns out that many humans hear just as well, if not slightly better, than do owls. So, even though there is no question that owls see and hear better than most

This fledgling northern saw-whet owl awaits a meal from its parents. The saw-whet is the smallest owl in the prairies, standing barely 20 centimeters (8 in.) tall.

The rose-breasted grosbeak ranges along the eastern edge of the prairies. It uses its seed-cracking bill to also feed on beetles and grasshoppers.

The great horned owl is normally active only at night. In winter, when cold weather taxes the bird's energy reserves, it may hunt in the late afternoon as this one is doing.

The secretive bobcat is about twice the size of the average domestic cat but is more muscular and weighs up to 12 kilograms (26 lb).

Newborn red foxes appear for the first time at the mouth of their natal burrow when they are about four weeks old.

diurnal birds, their sensory abilities in these areas are not much greater than our own.

A great horned owl may be as much as five times heavier than a long-eared owl, and this difference is reflected in the prey each hunts. The long-eared owl is primarily a small-mammal specialist, hunting young ground squirrels, voles, deer mice, pocket mice (*Perognathus* spp.), kangaroo rats, bats (*Myotis* spp.), and even small weasels (*Mustela* spp.). They occasionally also hunt songbirds and small snakes.

In contrast, the great horned owl hunts much larger prey and is a threat to many furred and feathered creatures on the prairies. This large, powerful owl hunts cottontails, jackrabbits, pocket gophers, ground squirrels, muskrats (*Ondatra zibethicus*), red fox pups, and perhaps even Fluffy, the unwary house cat. The nauseating spray of the striped skunk is also no protection from this taloned terror of the coulees, and the owls commonly hunt Pepe Le Pew. Remarkably, the owl will even attack and kill porcupines. One audacious owl that was examined by researchers had eighty-four quills in its face, sides, and legs.

The versatile great horned owl also hunts ducks, coots (*Fulica americana*), ring-necked pheasants (*Phasianus colchicus*), ruffed grouse, crows (*Corvus brachyrhynchos*), American bitterns (*Botaurus lentiginosus*), and even great blue herons (*Ardea herodias*). On the northern prairies, these rapacious owls also kill and eat peregrine falcons (*Falco peregrinus*), as well as short-eared owls (*Asio flammeus*), burrowing owls, red-tailed hawks, and sometimes even its neighbor, the long-eared owl.

The prey of both owls are not without their own defences, and these include cryptic coloration, quick reflexes, wariness, sensitive hearing, fetid sprays, and barbed quills. As we've seen, these defences are not always effective. Predators and prey are constantly evolving new adaptations to thwart each other. They are involved in an "arms race," with the predators developing new and better capture techniques and the prey, in turn, developing strategies to foil these techniques. This competition has led to highly honed predators and equally honed prey.

NIGHTWINGS

Bats, with 925 species worldwide, rank second after rodents as the most diverse group of mammals on Earth. They're primarily creatures of the tropics and subtropics, yet roughly three dozen species occur in North America, of which fewer than ten risk life on the northern prairies. Roughly half the species of prairie bats live in colonies in abandoned buildings, caves, and mines; the others, which include the hoary bat (*Lasiurus cinereus*), red bat (*L. borealis*), and western small-footed myotis (*Myotis ciliolabrum*), are generally solitary and spend the day in coulees, hanging among the foliage of trees, under bark, or in hollow trunks.

Bats have a number of features that distinguish them from birds. They use no nest, and the naked young of many species cling to their mother and accompany her on nightly hunting forays until they are old enough to be left alone. While insect-eating birds, such as tree swallows (*Tachycineta bicolor*) and nighthawks, catch their flying prey with their mouths, bats trap prey with the naked membrane between their legs and tail, which folds forward like a baseball mitt. Common to both bats and birds is the ability to digest food quickly and pass it rapidly through their intestines. This reduces the weight they carry in flight.

Tropical bats eat fruit, nectar, frogs, lizards, fish, and the blood of mammals and birds, as well as other bats. All prairie bats are insect eaters, and they use sonar to track and capture prey, such as moths, beetles, and flies. As the bats fly, they emit a series of supersonic clicks that reflects off insects and other objects and gives the bat a radar picture of the world in front of it. This behavior is called *echolocation*. A hunting little brown bat (*Myotis lucifugus*) generates 20 clicks per second at frequencies between 40,000 and 80,000 cycles per second. When the bat locates a target, it clicks more rapidly, up to 200 times per second, and it may also switch to a higher frequency if it can. Some bats echolocate at frequencies as high as 200,000 cycles per second. Typically, humans can hear sounds up to 20,000 cycles per second, but are most sensitive to the range from 1,000 to 4,000 cycles per second.

High-frequency echolocation has two important advantages: good directional precision and the capacity to detect minute objects. Using its sonar, a little brown bat can detect an object 0.3 millimeters (1/100 in.) in size, roughly the thickness of two pages of this book. But the use of high-frequency ultrasounds has a disadvantage; their range is exceedingly short. This means a bat must be very close to its prey to detect it. The weakness in the system works to the advantage of certain species of owlet moths (Family Noctuidae) that are preyed upon by bats. The moths can hear the supersonic clicks of a bat before the bat detects them with its sonar. The insects immediately abandon their usual cruising flight and go into sharp dives or erratic loops. The moths can detect the bat's high-frequency sounds with ears located on the sides of their thorax. Each ear is externally visible as a small cavity in which there is a transparent eardrum. The ears in most moths are solely for the detection of bats since the insects themselves make no sounds. If you jingle a set of car

These little brown bats huddle together in a winter hibernaculum. During hibernation, their body temperature drops to 2°Centigrade (36°F.), and frost may coat their fur.

keys near owlet moths fluttering around a porch light, the moths will take evasive action. The keys generate some high-frequency sounds that are inaudible to us but detectable to the moths and fool them into thinking they are being targeted by a hungry bat.

Some species of preying mantises (Order Mantodea), as well as some green lacewings (*Chrysopa* spp.), have also evolved bat-detecting ears. The mantids have a single ear between their hind legs, and the lacewings have one on each of their forewings. Some tiger moths (Family Arctiidae) not only hear the clicks of bats, but fight back by producing a train of their own high-frequency clicks. Researchers speculate that the ultrasonic counterattack by the moths may serve two purposes. It may jam the bat's sonar, or it may tell the bat what kind of moth it has in its sights. Brightly colored tiger moths are filled with distasteful chemicals and bats find them unpalatable. By signaling the bat, the moth averts a potentially lethal attack.

The bat-and-moth story has yet another twist. Tiny parasitic mites live in the ears of some owlet moths, impairing their ability to hear. If both ears become infested, the moths become deaf. This would not serve the mites well, as they would die along with their host when a bat made a meal of the moth. The mites climb aboard the moths when they visit a flower, and a moth may be parasitized numerous times from different flowers, yet all the mites settle into the same ear and leave the other one alone. Scientists believe that the first mite lays down an odor trail that all subsequent mites follow.

Bats live in a different sensory world from ours, a world we are only beginning to understand. With sophisticated auditory equipment we can now listen to their calls, and image intensifiers allow us to observe and photograph them under the faint glimmer of starlight. I have no doubt that, in time, unimagined technology will uncover other wondrous secrets and enrich the story of bats with further intrigue and complexities.

GEESE GOING DAYS

Aboriginal peoples kept track of time by observing the cycles of Nature, and the passage from one season to the next was often marked by the movements of animals. Cackling Canada geese (*Branta canadensis*) wedging across an October sky marked the return of autumn, the season when coulees ignite with color.

The shimmering golds of aspens that cloak the bottoms of autumn coulees and the rich ambers of cottonwoods that skirt the banks of rivers result from pigments that were always present but are masked during the growing season. Within every leaf there is a blend of colorful substances. Day length, temperature, and rainfall determine which of these colorful substances dominate in the different seasons. In spring and summer, the most abundant substance is the pigment *chlorophyll*, which imparts the green color to foliage. Chlorophyll is vital to plants; it captures the sun's energy and uses it to manufacture simple sugars that are the basis of the plant's nutrition. Sunlight is also required for the synthesis of chlorophyll itself. During the growing season, when days are long and sunlight is plentiful, chlorophyll is synthesized continually, and as long as the supply remains high, the leaves stay green. In autumn, the diminishing hours of daylight and the

The spectacular
blossoms of the
yellow lady's slipper
appear in June.
The flowers are
pollinated mainly
by bees, which are
attracted to the
flowers by their
color and fragrance.

cool temperatures slow the rate at which chlorophyll is produced. As the amount of chlorophyll dwindles inside the leaf, its masking effect fades and other colorful substances begin to show through.

One group of hidden substances is the *carotenoids*, yellow pigments that confer the Midas touch to aspens, cottonwoods, alders (*Alnus* spp.), birches (*Betula* spp.), and Manitoba maples. Carotenoids, unlike chlorophyll, do not need sunlight for their synthesis, and they are unaffected by the shortening days of autumn.

The reds and purples of coulee red osier dogwoods (*Cornus stolonifera*) and other shrubs result from the presence of another group of pigments called *anthocyanins*. Unlike the carotenoids, these pigments are not present throughout the growing season; they develop only in late summer as a result of a change in the metabolism of sugars. Anthocyanins give the rich color to many prairie fruits, such as pin cherries (*Prunus pensylvanica*), strawberries (*Fragaria glauca*), raspberries (*Rubus strigosus*), saskatoons (*Amelanchier alnifolia*), and rose hips (*Rosa* spp.).

Some autumns are more colorful than others. When rainfall is scanty, leaves may fade, turn brown, and fall from the tree with only a hint of color. Rainfall alone, however, does not guarantee a better display. If rains are heavy and combined with wind, the trees may be stripped of their foliage before the color peaks. The best conditions are warm, sunny days and cool nights without frost. Many believe that frost is a necessary ingredient for good autumn color, whereas, in fact, frost may kill the leaf and cause it to fall off prematurely.

Leaves are lost in autumn because it is the most economical way for a tree to survive the winter. Leaves continually lose water through surface pores that are open to absorb carbon dioxide for the manufacture of sugar. The manufacture of sugar ceases when the temperature becomes cold, and if the tree were to retain its leaves, it would continue to lose moisture without any benefit. Moreover, once the ground is

The paper wasp gathers fibers from the stems of weeds, the dry wood of dead trees, exposed boards, or discarded paper and mixes them with water to fashion its papery hive.

frozen, the tree cannot extract water from the soil to replenish its losses. Deciduous trees drain 95 percent of the minerals and other nutrients from their leaves before they are cast off, and they store these materials for the next growing season.

In late summer, a corky layer of cells forms at the base of each leaf stem. These cells prevent the passage of minerals, water, and other nutrients from the roots to the leaves and vice versa. This layer gradually weakens the attachment of the leaf, and eventually the wind snaps the leaf free.

The meandering course of the Milk River creates protected clusters of trees and shrubbery where wildlife can hide in the coulee bottom.

Sloughs with large stands of cattails offer sheltered nesting sites for many prairie birds, including ducks, grebes, bitterns, night herons, marsh wrens, Franklin's gulls, and Forster's terns.

SLOUGHS WATER AND WINGS

PHOTOGRAPHING IN PRAIRIE SLOUGHS TAKES A SPECIAL BRAND OF DEDICATION. IN MY EARLY YEARS, I COULDN'T AFFORD EXPENSIVE BOOTS SO I SIMPLY ACCEPTED THAT TO GET WET AND COLD WAS THE PRICE ONE PAID TO PHOTOGRAPH IN SUCH AREAS. EVENTUALLY, I BOUGHT SOME CHEST WADERS.

The male yellow-headed blackbird growls and rattles the most unmusical of calls. His vocal charm may convince as many as eight females to nest in his territory.

These were fine for a while, until I got mired several times and had to waddle to shore with more water inside the boots than out. The current solution? A black rubber wetsuit. I love to watch the facial expressions on passing motorists as I explode from the cattails beside a prairie highway, dressed in clinging black neoprene and wearing a mosquito head net. Usually, I find the drivers pulled over for a rest a few kilometers up the road.

The general rolling topography of the northern prairies results in millions of natural depressions. When these depressions fill with water, they are called sloughs. These vital prairie wetlands are most abundant in the rolling landscape of southeastern Alberta, southern Saskatchewan, southwestern Manitoba, and eastern North and South Dakota, where they contribute to the beauty and diversity of the mixed grasslands.

Sloughs are different than small lakes and ponds. They have no streams draining into or out of them, and they receive all of their water as runoff in spring. Many sloughs dry up in summer, and in the driest regions of the grasslands, a third of them disappear by mid-July. The transient nature of some sloughs, however, does not seem to discourage their use by wildlife. Prairie sloughs are the "duck factory" of the continent. Over 50 percent of all ducks in North America and 80 percent of all redheads (*Aythya americana*), canvasbacks (*Aythya valisineria*), northern pintails (*Anas acuta*), and mallards (*Anas platyrhynchos*) start life on a prairie slough. Sloughs also attract red-winged and yellow-headed blackbirds (*Agelaius phoeniceus* and *Xanthocephalus xanthocephalus*), grebes (*Podiceps* spp.), herons, bitterns, avocets (*Recurvirostra americana*), and willets (*Catoptrophorus semipalmatus*), and they are essential in the reproductive cycle of grassland frogs and toads. They also serve as feeding and resting areas for migrating waterfowl and shorebirds in spring and fall.

Even though many sloughs are shallow and transient, they are often more productive of wildlife than the permanent lakes found farther north in the boreal forest and in the arctic tundra. Sloughs are rich in nutrients washed in by surface drainage. These nutrients are concentrated by evaporation, and the resulting high fertility encourages the proliferation of invertebrates, algae, duckweeds, and pondweeds that nourish wildlife. The lakes of the boreal forest and tundra, in contrast, are frequently acidic and commonly produce only a tenth as many invertebrates per volume of water as do prairie sloughs. Moreover, ducks like to be spaced apart, so many tiny sloughs are better than a single large lake.

One characteristic of sloughs is that they differ, sometimes dramatically. Some sloughs are ringed with bulrushes (*Scirpus* spp.) and cattails (*Typha latifolia*); others have a perimeter of willows and aspens; some have a "bathtub" ring of white alkali salt with an outer ring of snowberry and rose shrubs; and still others seem to have no vegetation at all surrounding them. Sloughs can be large or tiny, although the average size is 0.5 hectares (1.2 acres), and deep or shallow, but those with less than 40 centimeters (16 in.) of water are generally dry by midsummer.

All sloughs are transitional and always in a process of change. The change may be rapid, or exceedingly slow,

The female American bittern, alone, builds the family nest of reeds, rushes, and cattails, incubates the eggs, and broods and feeds the fuzzy-headed chicks.

The seeds of the bur-reed are a valuable food for prairie ducks, rails, and snipe, and the entire plant is eaten by muskrats.

This slough in Sheyenne National Grasslands in North Dakota was an important breeding wetland for boreal chorus frogs, tiger salamanders, and Canadian toads.

depending upon a number of factors. Ultimately, every slough is destined to disappear, though possibly not for thousands of years. Each will eventually be filled with sediments and converted to grasslands, the climax habitat of the mixed-grass prairie. If we follow a typical slough through a succession of stages, it is possible to understand why sloughs often look so different from one another and how the plants and animals that inhabit them change with time.

THE EVOLUTION OF A SLOUGH

The first stage in the life of a slough is the *pioneer* stage, when mud on the bottom is barren of plant life. This stage was common to all sloughs at the end of the last glaciation, when the ice retreated from the northern prairie region. The earliest colonizers of a slough are microscopic plants and animals, carried on the legs of birds that inadvertently seed the water. The rich minerals, warm water temperatures, and sunshine lead to a proliferation of these minute organisms, which grow, reproduce, die, and settle on the bottom of the slough, adding to its fertility and building up a layer of organic muck.

In the pioneer stage, waterfowl use the slough as loafing and preening areas. During grooming, seeds of pondweeds (*Potamogeton* spp.) and filamentous algae are knocked loose from the birds' feathers and legs and root in the oozy material on the bottom of the slough. The roots of these submerged plants bind the ooze together, and when the plants die, they add to the accumulating material. At this stage, snails (Class Gastropoda), mayflies (Order Ephemeroptera), scarlet water mites (Superfamily Hydracarina), and numerous other invertebrates appear, transported by animals, birds, and the wind.

As organic matter gradually settles on the bottom, the slough gets shallower. In the next stage, the *floating aquatic* stage, plants such as white and yellow watercrowfoot (*Ranunculus* spp.) and common bladderwort (*Utricularia vulgaris*) take root. Their floating leaves shelter a host of new residents, including boreal chorus frogs (*Pseudacris maculata*), tiger salamanders (*Ambystoma tigrinum*), diving beetles (*Dytiscus* spp.), and dozens of other insects. As the leaves spread over the surface of the slough, they prevent sunlight from reaching the depths, and the underwater pondweeds struggle to photosynthesize. Eventually, the shadowed plants die and add their tissues to the bottom ooze. The fertile muck now supports a rich bottom fauna of dragonfly larvae (Order Odonata), predacious water tigers (*Dytiscus* spp.), roundworms (Phylum Nematoda), and blood-sucking leeches (Class Hirudinea). Once, and only once, did I sit in a blind with my bare feet planted in the bottom ooze of a slough. Unknown to me, within that ooze lurked formidable jaws, and I suffered for a week with swollen, bitten feet that itched incessantly.

The floating aquatic plants of the slough need the buoyancy of water, and they disappear first along the water's edge. Once the shallow shoreline fills with sediment, there is not enough water to support their soft stems. Another group of wetland plants, the *emergents*, move in and fill the void. These plants have strong, flexible stems and narrow leaves that bend easily before the wind and water. The emergent plants partition the shallow water; bulrushes, cattails, and sedges (*Carex* spp.) grow farthest from shore, and closer in grow the water smartweeds (*Polygonum amphibium*), arrowheads (*Sagittaria cuneata*), rushes (*Juncus* spp.), and spike-rushes (*Eleocharis* spp.). In the evolution of a slough, this is called the *emergent* stage. Numerous ducks, black-crowned night-herons (*Nycticorax nycticorax*), flamboyant blackbirds, and loquacious marsh wrens (*Cistothorus palustris*) become its conspicuous residents, feeding and nesting among the forest of emergent stems.

When a slough is deep and survives for years, willows may form a partial or complete margin around the water. The shrubs break the wind and lessen the losses to evaporation. In winter, snow piles up around the bushes, and greater amounts of meltwater rejuvenate the slough the following spring.

Back in the center of the slough, another story is unfolding. As aquatic vegetation continues to grow, the water becomes depleted of oxygen from the decay of accumulating bottom debris. In summer, warm water temperatures accelerate the decay and aggravate the oxygen shortage even more. At this stage, only animals with low oxygen requirements find the bottom habitable. Meanwhile, the march of the emergent plants continues, their dense, fibrous roots securing the shoreline position. Eventually, a time comes when much of the old open-water area is covered by bulrushes, with an outer rim of cattails and sedges.

The evolution of a slough is not always the steady progression I've outlined so far. Topography, climate, erosion, and the effects of wildlife and livestock combine to dictate its evolution, which can be fast or slow, steady or stuttered, backward or forward. A slough may move rapidly forward through several stages and then become stalled in a stage for centuries, before finally reverting back to an earlier stage. In wet years, the submerged and floating aquatic plants may flourish, whereas in years of drought, the emergent cattails and bulrushes may dominate.

As the bottom rises, the slough dries up in summer and becomes temporary and seasonal, as are a third of sloughs in the mixed grasslands. Then, only animals, such as insects, that can withstand drying in summer and freezing in winter persist. The surrounding grasses begin to advance and reclaim the area.

The water in sloughs is often salty because it is fed by heavily mineralized runoff. High evaporation rates further concentrate the salts. When sloughs dry up, the salts remain: calcium sulfate (gypsum), magnesium sulfate (Epsom salts), and sodium sulfate (Glauber's salts). Most grasses and other plants cannot survive in salty soil because the soil draws water out of the plant, and the plant withers and dies. One group of plants, called *halophytes*, are able to increase the salt concentration within their own tissues beyond the concentration of salts in the soil and, therefore, draw in water and survive. This stage in the evolution of a slough, the one dominated by halophytes, is called the *saline grassland* stage. The salt concentration is highest in the center of the old slough where the water disappeared last, and it decreases gradually toward the outside edge. Since halophytes vary in their ability to tolerate salts, concentric bands of vegetation form, with the most salt-tolerant species in the center and the least-tolerant species at the periphery, where they merge with the usual mixed grasses of the region. In the center of a saline grassland is red samphire (*Salicornia rubra*) and seaside arrowgrass (*Triglochin maritima*); next is salt grass (*Distichlis stricta*); and on the outside is foxtail barley (*Hordeum jubatum*) and northern and western wheat grass (*Agropyron dasystachyum* and *A. smithii*).

As the saline grassland ages, generations of halophytes die and build up the soil, and the scanty annual rainfall slowly leaches out the salts. Eventually, the halophytes are replaced by the usual spectrum of mixed grasses, and the *climax* stage is reached.

SPINELESS WONDERS

At every stage in the life of a slough, the most abundant wild creatures are insects. Insects are the most successful terrestrial animals on Earth, comprising 85 percent of all known species. Researchers estimate that the weight of insects on the planet may be six times greater than the total weight of all humanity. The rich fertile waters of the prairie slough attract a fascinating array of insect inhabitants, some secretive and submerged, others colorful and conspicuous.

Dozens of species of mosquitoes (Family Culicidae) have been identified from the sloughs of the northern grasslands. Because of their roles as vectors in many human diseases worldwide, these bloodthirsty little demons have been studied extensively, and their natural history is well known.

All mosquitoes begin life as an egg in a puddle, often a dirty, stagnant puddle. The eggs may hatch along the shoreline of a vast prairie slough, in a flooded ditch, in a discarded rubber tire, even inside an empty beer can. Only female mosquitoes have a thirst for blood; the males feed on nectar and plant juices. Females

Dragonfly nymphs are completely aquatic and breathe through gills in their rectum. With their final molt they emerge as the familiar winged air-breathing predators.

The male northern harrier sometimes adds sticks to the family nest, but he rarely incubates the eggs. He does, however, do all the hunting for himself and his mate throughout incubation.

will also sip sap for energy, but they need the protein and fats in a sanguineous meal to produce an ample batch of eggs. Most species of mosquito feed on just one group of hosts, either reptiles, birds, or mammals. The problem is that some mosquitoes don't always behave as they should, as evidenced by the recent emergence of West Nile virus. This virulent disease is infectious to many kinds of birds, but crows are particularly susceptible. The disease can be transmitted to humans by a bite from a mosquito that has fed on an infected bird. The disease first appeared in New York City in the summer of 1999. By the summer of 2003, it had arrived in the prairies.

As you stroll around a prairie slough on a warm summer evening, it's hard to believe that mosquitoes are interested in anything other than humans. Different species feed at different times of the day, so it is possible to be punctured (pricked or stabbed would be better) in the morning by one species, riddled at noon by others, feasted upon at dusk by yet another, and attacked at nightfall by several more. Mosquitoes are attracted to us by the plume of carbon dioxide we exhale with each breath. They have sensors in their antennae that can detect this gas from as far away as 80 meters (260 ft.) away. So, what's my suggestion? I have none, except to keep rooting for dragonflies, the mosquitoes' worst nightmare.

Dragonflies are common, conspicuous inhabitants of the slough. Colored in vibrant greens, golds, and reds, they have fanciful names such as cherry-faced meadowhawk (*Sympetrum internum*), four-spotted skimmer (*Libellula quadrimaculata*), and pale snaketail (*Ophiogomphus severus*). All are fast-flying slayers of the slough that prey on other insects, especially mosquitoes, grinding up three hundred or more in a day and earning them the nickname "mosquito hawk." Dragonflies catch their victims on the wing, and for this they need good vision. One of the most conspicuous features of a dragonfly is its large, compound eyes. Compound eyes cannot be closed, moved, or focused, as ours can, but they are better for detecting movement, and they can

see in many directions at the same time. Many insects have compound eyes, but they are biggest and best in the dragonfly.

A compound eye is composed of thousands of long, cylindrical units, called *ommatidia*, each of which receives light and produces an image. The number of ommatidia is a reflection of how the insect lives. For example, a honey bee (*Apis mellifera*) has 4,000 ommatidia in each eye, and a swallowtail butterfly (*Papilio* spp.) has 17,000. Both the bee and the butterfly feed on flowers that are stationary and usually conspicuously colored. The predatory dragonfly has 28,000 ommatidia. Because its prey are small and fast flying, it needs eyes that are especially sensitive to movement.

Two other insects that live in sloughs, the whirligig beetle (Family Gyrinidae) and the water strider (Family Gerridae), can't seem to make up their minds whether to live in air or in water, so they live at the interface between the two. At the surface of any body of water, the water molecules are not attracted evenly from all sides, so the surface responds like a stretched membrane that can support objects. This surface tension allows water striders and whirligig beetles to skate on water.

The whirligig beetle is a round, black beetle that can dive or fly, but it usually plows through the surface film half in and half out of the water. Its compound eyes are actually divided, with the lower half recording events underwater and the upper half searching the sky. It skims about the surface, erratically searching for luckless insects that fall on the water. Its antennae, which rest on the water's surface, detect ripples reflected from objects in its path so it can swerve and avoid them. Its swift reflexes allow dozens, and sometimes hundreds, of whirligigs to swim together in a dense cluster, called a *raft*, on the same patch of slough without a single collision.

The water strider lives on the surface of the water, rowing with its middle pair of long legs. Its feet are covered with unwettable hairs that support its weight on the elastic surface film. When an insect, such as a mosquito larva, comes to the surface for air, the strider stabs the wiggler with its sharp mouthparts and injects digestive saliva. It then sucks out the liquefied contents, and the empty shell of the victim drifts to the bottom of the slough.

Water striders will hide when you approach the edge of a slough, but they are much more sensitive to vibrations on the water surface. Striders detect these vibrations with sensors in their legs. They use ripples in the water to communicate ownership, courtship, and aggression. When a male strider is floating next to a leaf, a feather, or a piece of wood, he taps on the water and sends out a message with a specific frequency of ripples intended to attract a mate. Once a female is lured closer, the male switches to a different pattern of ripples with a faster frequency. When she finally moves to within a few centimeters of him, he switches to his special courtship ripple pattern—something no female strider seems able to resist. The male uses a different sequence of ripples to aggressively defend his territory and his mate from other rippling Romeos. Numerous species of water strider may live in the same slough, and each uses its own unique repertoire of ripple patterns.

The scarlet epaulets on the male red-winged blackbird are a badge of ownership and are displayed most conspicuously when the bird sings its territorial song.

SONGSTERS OF THE SLOUGH

Courtship brings out the talkativeness in many animals, and some of the most loquacious in their pursuit of carnal gratification are the frogs and toads, who never say a word until it is time to mate.

In the evolution of life, amphibians (frogs, toads, and salamanders) followed fish. They developed a strengthened skeleton to support them away from the buoyancy of water and lungs to breathe air. But amphibians never became completely emancipated from water, as did the later-evolving reptiles, birds, and mammals. The amphibians' dependence on water is most apparent when you consider their sex lives. Frogs and toads court, mate, and lay their eggs in water, and they spend the early phase of their lives as aquatic tadpoles. Six species of frogs and toads live in the arid northern prairies: the plains spadefoot toad (*Spea bombifrons*), the Canadian toad (*Bufo hemiophrys*), the American toad (*Bufo americanus*), the Great Plains toad (*Bufo cognatus*), the northern leopard frog (*Rana pipiens*), and the boreal chorus frog (*Pseudacris maculata*). Of the six, the most conspicuous is the boreal chorus frog, whose loud springtime serenades are a delightful decree of spring's arrival on the northern prairies.

The boreal chorus frog is the smallest of the frogs and toads on the prairies and has a total length of just 2 to 4 centimeters (0.8 to 1.6 in.). Breeding occurs from early April to June, often beginning before the snow melts. This tiny frog has a surprisingly loud, penetrating call for its size. My friend Bruce Caywood lives beside a slough, and in the springtime, these frogs sing so loudly at night that he has to raise the volume on his television, something he's happy to do. The distinctive call of the chorus frog can be mimicked by running a fingernail along the teeth of a small, plastic comb.

Chorus frogs will breed in almost any body of water, deep or shallow, but their greatest numbers occur in sloughs. The males, who do all the singing, gather along the edges of the water or around flooded tufts of vegetation. Each songster calls from his own tiny territory. The songs of all frogs are unique to each species, and they differ in frequency, duration, and the number of notes. The hearing of female frogs is most

The nocturnal tiger salamander is a rarely seen inhabitant of deeper sloughs and dugouts. Adults can be 18 centimeters (7 in.) long and feed on insects, earthworms, and molluscs.

sensitive to the frequencies of their own species, and they hear the calls of their own males best, even when three or four species of amphibians may be calling in the same slough on the same night.

Frogs are perfunctory lovers. They have dispensed with elaborate courtship displays and foreplay in favor of the croak-and-grab approach. A calling male does not discriminate and will grab any frog that comes into his territory, including other males and frogs of other species. In cases of misidentification, the "grabbee" immediately notifies the "grabber" with a grunt, and the grabbee is released. In the sexual embrace of frogs, called *amplexus*, the male chorus frog jumps on the back of the female and clasps her behind the front legs. The males have a special roughened pad on the first finger of their front feet that helps them hold the female during mating. The eggs are laid beneath the surface of the water in clumps of vegetation. This buffers them against the cold air and protects them in case a skim of ice forms. The female chorus frog may lay up to fifteen hundred eggs over the course of a couple of days. Throughout it all, the male sticks to the female's back, flooding the eggs with sperm each time she lays.

The eggs hatch in from ten days to two weeks, and the tadpoles, smaller than a grain of rice, take two months to grow and transform into tiny froglets. Most chorus frogs breed in waters where there are no fish to prey on them. Even so, the tadpoles are hunted by diving beetles (*Dytiscus* spp.), giant water bugs (*Lethocerus americanus*), and other invertebrate predators. The transformation from an aquatic, gill-breathing, vegetarian tadpole to a terrestrial, lung-breathing, carnivorous adult frog is one of the most remarkable phenomena in the life of any frog. Under the influence of the thyroid gland, the round mouth of the tadpole widens and develops a tongue, and the rows of rasping teeth it used to feed on algae are shed. Nostrils and lungs appear and the external gills slowly shrink. Limbs gradually lengthen and the tail is absorbed. The metamorphosis is orderly and exquisitely timed so that the swimming tail does not shrink before the jumping legs have grown.

Once the breeding season is over, chorus frogs seem to disappear, and little is known about their behavior. The adults feed on insects, millipedes, and snails, hunting in marshy areas and damp woods. Most die before winter, having bred only once.

THE SMELLY WATER RAT

The muskrat (*Ondatra zibethicus*) gets its name from the male's strong, musky odor during the spring breeding season. A pair of glands near the end of the animal's penis exudes a strong-smelling, yellowish secretion that mixes with its urine and is dabbed on defecation posts, along travel routes, and on lodges to advertise his machismo. The female has similar glands on her clitoris, but they are less active. This is probably more information than you want to know, but it could be a lifesaving source of conversation at some tedious cocktail gathering.

The muskrat is a common resident of many large permanent sloughs in the northern prairies. The slough must be at least a meter (3 ft.) deep so that the water does not freeze to the bottom in winter, and there should be lots of bulrushes, sedges, pondweeds, and especially cattails, the muskrat's favorite food.

Muskrats live in lodges or bank burrows. A burrow may have a short tunnel with room for only one animal or be an elaborate maze of passageways and chambers extending up to 100 meters (328 ft.) from the water's edge. Burrows are used especially in summer because they are cool and secure.

Unlike the beaver, which occupies a lodge year round, the muskrat builds a house just for the winter. Starting in September,

Muskrats are active throughout the prairie winter, foraging daily for the underwater root stalks of cattails, bulrushes, and reeds.

The mink is a shoreline predator hunting rodents and small birds on the water's edge and crustaceans, frogs, and small fish in the shallows.

the industrious rodent stacks cattails (*Typha latifolia*), bulrushes (*Scirpus* spp.), pondweeds (*Potamogeton* spp.), and mud into a conical mound up to 1.2 meters (4 ft.) high at the edge of its marshy domain. At the same time as it builds its winter lodge, it also builds a number of feeding shelters nearby. These shelters resemble a lodge, only are smaller, about half the size. After the ice forms, the muskrat builds a third kind of shelter, called a *pushup*. The toothy rodent gnaws a hole through the ice, then stuffs soggy vegetation up under the snow where it freezes and forms a small cavity where the animal can rest and eat. All of these shelters are spaced close enough together so that the muskrat never exceeds its breath-holding capacity, which is just 58 seconds. In that time, a muskrat can swim underwater about 46 meters (151 ft.) before it runs out of air. Veteran muskrat researcher Dr. Robert MacArthur observed: "... pushups and feeding shelters are often arranged about a central dwelling lodge in a stepping-stone pattern. Thus the residents have access to all points in their home range via a series of short underwater excursions."

DIVERS AND DABBLERS

Prairie ducks can be divided into two broad categories: divers and dabblers. Watching how a particular duck feeds and how it takes flight will allow you to distinguish between the two groups. Typically, divers stay in the open water in the middle of the slough and dive completely underwater when searching for food. Dabblers usually paddle along the edges and skim food off the top of the water or else tip their bottoms up to reach food just below the surface.

The prairie dabblers include the familiar mallard (*Anas platyrhynchos*), the northern pintail, northern shoveler (*Anas clypeata*), blue-winged teal (*A. discors*), green-winged teal (*A. crecca*), cinnamon teal (*A. cyanoptera*), gadwall (*A. strepera*), and American

The comblike fringe along the inside edge of a northern shoveler's bill is the finest of any prairie duck. Because of this, it can strain the smallest of seeds and aquatic invertebrates.

widgeon (*A. americana*). The legs on all of these ducks are near the center of their bodies, so when they take off, they jump straight into the air and are gone. On land, the dabblers walk with a characteristic waddle.

When it comes time to build a nest, the dabblers waddle and flap as far as 1.6 kilometers (1 mi.) away from the slough. They hide their nests among uncropped grasses, along fence rows, or in clumps of snowberry, rose, and silverberry (*Elaeagnus commutata*).

To lessen competition in the shallow water where dabblers gather, they feed in slightly different ways on slightly different foods. For example, pintails feed closest to shore, mostly on aquatic invertebrates: snails, crustaceans, fly larvae, water boatmen, and earthworms. Gadwalls and widgeons dabble a little farther from shore, searching for the seeds and stems of grasses, sedges, rushes, and pondweeds. All prairie dabbling ducks have a comblike fringe along the edge of their upper and lower beak, which they use to strain food from the water. The northern shoveler has the finest straining system of all the dabblers and, consequently, feeds on the smallest foods: shrimps, snails, and copepods, as well as an assortment of tiny seeds.

The prairie diving ducks include the canvasback, redhead, lesser scaup (*Aythya affinis*), and ruddy duck (*Oxyura jamaicensis*). As their name suggests, these ducks usually dive completely underwater when searching for food, and their legs are located closer to the rear of their bodies, which gives them more power and steering ability. When a diving duck takes off, it runs across the surface of the water to build up speed before it becomes airborne. On land, their walk is clumsy, and they prefer to rest on the water rather than on shore with the

Formerly, the Sweetgrass Hills in northern Montana were home to grizzly bears and wolves that ranged out onto the prairies and along river valleys.

dabblers. The diving ducks also differ from dabblers in their nesting biology, building their nests within the thick cattails and bulrushes surrounding the slough rather than at a distance.

When foraging, the diving ducks also partition the slough to reduce competition. The canvasback and redhead illustrate how subtle the partitioning can be. Both are diving ducks that commonly feed in open water up to 3 meters (9.8 ft.) deep, but when necessary, the slightly larger and heavier canvasback can dive to depths of 10 meters (33 ft.). The bill structure of the two ducks also differs. The redhead's beak is better designed to strain aquatic insects, while that of the canvasback is specialized to sieve plant foods. Finally, the two ducks regularly feed at different levels in the water column. Canvasbacks plunge to the bottom, tear out roots and tubers, and strain the mud for seeds. Redheads feed more on submerged stems and leaves from mid-water levels.

Even though ducks live in water, their skin never gets wet. They keep their plumage waterproof by applying oil to their feathers. When preening, a duck repeatedly rubs its head and bill on the base of its back. This is the location of its preen gland, which produces an oily, waxy secretion that is fastidiously spread over all of its plumage. The preen gland is largest in aquatic birds, and ducks may preen as often as seventeen times a day. When young ducklings hatch, mother ducks preen even more, as frequently as several times an hour. A possible explanation is that oil is spread from the adult's plumage to the downy young, although young ducklings instinctively perform preening movements when only a day old. The oily secretions not only keep a duck's feathers healthy and waterproof, but also keep its legs and bill from drying out.

DEVIL DIVERS

If you love grebes, as I do, then the grasslands are for you. Six of the seven grebe species found in North America make their homes in the sloughs of the northern prairies: red-necked grebe (*Podiceps grisegena*), eared grebe (*P. nigricollis*), horned grebe (*P. auritus*), pied-billed grebe (*Podilymbus podiceps*), western grebe (*Aechmophorus occidentalis*), and Clark's grebe (*A. clarkii*). Grebes are water birds that are frequently mistaken for ducks, but they are altogether different. Whereas a duck's bill is blunt and flattened for sifting through mud and plant material, the grebe's bill is slim and pointed for feeding on aquatic beetles, larvae, worms, crustaceans, tadpoles, and tiger salamanders. Grebes are superlative divers, and their legs are positioned farther to the rear of their bodies than in any of the diving ducks. As well, their feathers trap less air, their bones are more solid, and their air sacs are smaller—features that make grebes less buoyant and better able to submerge. They can disappear underwater without a ripple, and the speed with which they can do this has earned them several colorful nicknames: "hell-diver," "water witch," and "devil diver."

If I were an egg, the first place I would choose to be laid would be in a duck's nest, and the last place would be in a grebe's nest. In a duck's nest I would be dry and nestled in fluffy, warm down. In a grebe's nest I would be wet, jostled, and dirty. All of the grebes build floating nests of decaying vegetation, and their eggs

This nesting eared grebe was just one of several hundred pairs nesting in a shallow slough smaller than the size of a football field.

often sit in water. On windy days, the water in sloughs can be whipped into waves that may capsize a nest and wash out the eggs. Grebes' eggs are whitish when they are first laid, but soon become stained brown from the fermenting vegetation. The single consolation in my life as a grebe's egg would be that when I hatch I could

During courtship, American avocets may sing a duet. The song sessions may occur sporadically while the pair is feeding.

ride on my parents' backs and clamber aboard anytime for a rest or for warmth.

Sloughs concentrate salts, so the water, vegetation, and invertebrate life are high in salt content. As a result, it's essential that grebes and other water birds living in sloughs excrete large amounts of salt, or face dehydration. For this purpose they have specialized glands located above the inside corner of each eye to eliminate excess salt from their blood. The salt glands become even more important for grebes on their wintering grounds along the Atlantic and Pacific coastlines, where they must eat marine invertebrates and drink salt water.

The eared, horned, and pied-billed grebes are the three smallest prairie grebes. Their ranges overlap extensively on the prairies, and you might predict that they would compete with each other. Since prairie ducks lessen competition by feeding on different foods, in different areas of the slough, perhaps grebes do the same. In fact, the grebes do feed on different fish on their marine wintering grounds, but there are no fish in prairie sloughs, and on their summer nesting grounds, the three species feed on the same insect and invertebrate life. It turns out that what the grebes do to lessen competition is to select different types of sloughs.

The eared grebe nests in groups, and it selects large, open sloughs for its colonies, which may contain several thousand pairs. The pied-billed grebe and the horned grebe are solitary nesters, and they settle on smaller sloughs. Usually, each slough has only one nesting pair. Although the horned and pied-billed grebes prefer the same size slough, they prefer different amounts of emergent vegetation to be present. Pied-billed grebes prefer heavily vegetated sloughs with thick stands of bulrushes and cattails. Horned grebes, on the other hand, need very little vegetation to satisfy them, sometimes nesting in completely open water on sloughs with no emergent vegetation at all. However, in such open-water situations, their nests are frequently swamped by waves and lost.

SUNSEEKERS

Every autumn, thousands of tiny yellow warblers (*Dendroica petechia*), each weighing less than 10 grams (0.4 oz.), fly more than 3,000 kilometers (1,860 mi.) to their wintering grounds in Mexico. For a human to achieve an equivalent feat would require traveling 2,400,000 kilometers (1,488,000 mi.), six times the distance from Earth to the moon.

Such lengthy migrations are common among the birds that summer in the temperate and higher latitudes of North America. Of the roughly 250 species of birds that fly the skies of the prairies, 85 percent migrate to more clement climes to avoid the rigors of a northern winter. But migration carries risks. Predators, human hunters, disorientation, starvation, dehydration, exhaustion, and collision with manmade structures exact a heavy toll. To offset the many risks of migration, birds accumulate surplus fuel in the form of fat, precisely time the moment of their departure, select a migration speed, altitude, and direction, and successfully navigate a lengthy course over largely unfamiliar terrain.

Shorebirds that nest in the Arctic—sandpipers (*Calidris* spp.), plovers (*Pluvialis* spp.), dowitchers (*Limnodromus* spp.), and phalaropes (*Phalaropus* spp.)—

Female Wilson's phalaropes are larger and more brightly colored than males. The females also do all the courting. Once the eggs are laid, they abandon their male partners who incubate the eggs and care for the chicks alone.

are the first migrants to revisit the slough in autumn on their journey south. These birds often pass through the prairies as early as August, long before inclement weather or a shortage of food compels them to leave their northern nesting grounds. An innate annual rhythm regulates many aspects of bird behavior, including the urge to migrate. In northern birds, this rhythm is modified and finely tuned by cues from the environment, especially the day length. The decreasing hours of daylight in late summer initiate restlessness in the birds and stimulate them to leave.

Shorebirds, as well as ducks, geese, gulls, terns, and grebes, migrate both day and night, but many other species are more selective. For example, many small, perching birds, such as warblers, vireos, thrushes, sparrows, and flycatchers, which normally live in thickly shrubby habitats, migrate only at night under the cover of darkness. By doing so, they avoid diurnal predators, such as raptors and gulls, and also leave the daylight hours free for foraging so they can restore their energy reserves. Nocturnal migration has other benefits as well. Cooler air means more lift, so less energy is needed for flight, and the birds also lose less moisture when they breathe, which lowers the risk of dehydration. Wind velocities are also usually lower at night so there are fewer problems from troublesome head winds.

Large, soaring birds, such as hawks, eagles, turkey vultures (*Cathartes aura*), white pelicans (*Pelecanus erythrorhynchos*), and sandhill cranes (*Grus canadensis*), migrate during the day. They rely on thermal updrafts to carry them aloft so they can conserve energy. By soaring, they burn at least three to four times less energy than if they flew by flapping. Thermals may carry these migrants as high as 6,000 meters (19,700 ft.). Then, at the top of the updraft, as the air cools and loses its lift, they glide away in the direction they wish to travel. From one updraft to another, the birds may circle and glide hundreds, and sometimes thousands, of kilometers southward.

Trumpeter swans pass through the prairies in April and October migrating to and from their northern nesting grounds.

Ten or eleven races of Canada geese occur in North America. The so-called "giant Canada" is the race that nests in the prairies, and ganders weigh an average 5.5 kilograms (12 lb.).

Many grassland migrants travel to the southern United States, Mexico, or Central America, but some fly as far as the tropics of South America. Although many birds break their journey into sections, with stopovers for feeding and resting, some geese may fly nonstop for 60 hours and cover 2,500 kilometers (1,550 mi.).

Two of the most distant migrants among prairie birds are the common nighthawk and Swainson's hawk (*Buteo swainsoni*), both of which commonly overwinter in northern Argentina, a round trip of 22,000 kilometers (13,640 mi.). For the Swainson's hawk, this is the longest migration flight of any member of the hawk family in North America. One female Swainson's hawk from Saskatchewan was tracked by satellites. She left Canada on 22 September and arrived in Argentina sixty-nine days later.

Birds live in an expanded sensory world compared to humans. Some birds can detect polarized and ultraviolet light and measure the angle of the sun. Others can sense changes in barometric pressure in advance of a storm, while some can hear the low-frequency sounds generated by thunderstorms, the jet stream, and pounding ocean surf. A few species may even sense the invisible force of Earth's magnetic field. Migrating birds use some or all of these cues to aid them in navigation.

Since birds have such good eyesight, it is reasonable to suppose that they use vision to navigate and that they might use celestial cues such as the sun, moon, and stars to guide them. In an intriguing series of experiments, it was shown that birds do indeed use the sun to orient themselves. Furthermore, they adjust for the changing angle of the sun throughout the day. To do this, they must possess an internal clock that accurately senses the passage of time. But many birds migrate at night when the sun is invisible. To prove that birds may use stars to navigate, cages were built in which the roofs contained rotating star maps. Consistently, the birds detected changes in positions of the stars and adjusted their direction appropriately. It has been known for a long time that birds recognize landmarks such as coastlines, mountain ranges, and large waterways and follow them in migration. More recent, however, is the discovery that a number of birds may sense Earth's magnetic field. It's possible these migrants have permanent magnets within their heads that work like a compass and help them navigate. Accumulations of magnetite, a magnetic material, have been found in the neck muscles and heads of white-crowned sparrows (*Zonotrichia leucophrys*), tree swallows (*Tachycineta bicolor*), western grebes, and northern pintails. This discovery is an exciting one, but in the final analysis, it will undoubtedly prove to be only one of many aids that avian sunseekers use to migrate.

A third of all prairie sloughs dry up by midsummer. Until then, they are important wetlands for wildlife.

The bullsnake is the largest snake in the northern prairies. It is a capable climber and will scale cottonwoods to hunt for nesting birds and roosting bats.

In 1979, Dinosaur
Provincial Park in
Alberta was selected
as a World Heritage
Site by the United
Nations Educational,
Scientific,
and Cultural
Organization
(UNESCO) in
recognition of
its outstanding
universal value as a
dinosaur fossil field
and a landscape
of unique physical
character.

BADLANDS LAYERS OF TIME

AS A PHOTOGRAPHER, I AM DRAWN TO THE BADLANDS BY THEIR GILDED HILLS AND EBONY SHADOWS. AS A
SCIENTIST, I AM DRAWN TO THEM BY THEIR RAW GEOLOGY AND THE TENACITY OF THE PLANT AND ANIMAL LIFE.
AND AS A HUMAN, I AM DRAWN TO THE BADLANDS BY THEIR GRANDEUR, A GRANDEUR THAT MAKES ME HUMBLE
AND FILLS ME WITH A COMFORTING SENSE OF INSIGNIFICANCE.

Most believe that early French trappers were the first to coin the name "badlands." They described the rugged topography flanking the White River in South Dakota as *mauvaises terres*, possibly because the area was difficult to traverse. The name could have also arisen out of the frustration of early settlers who found the rocky badlands impossible to farm. Whichever you believe, the badlands are still only "bad" from the viewpoint of humans. Within the mixed-grass prairies, the badlands are a separate habitat attracting a rich assemblage of plants and animals, possessed of a singular beauty, enticing and addicting in its ruggedness.

Blackfoot Natives came to the badlands to dream and seek visions, and outlaws came to hide from the noose. Within the deep valleys of the badlands, the fossilized bones of long extinct dinosaurs erupt from clay slopes, and in mid-July, when the heat is paralyzing, the land seems only to have its past, for nothing stirs. The badlands are one of my favorite prairie haunts. In the badlands, I drift and wander, for to introduce a pace or a purpose would lessen the experience. There, I have found secret nooks where I could rest and reflect on humanity's relationship with the grasslands. Humans are the product of four and a half billion years of fortuitous events, for some, the culmination of evolution. But there is nothing to suggest that the evolutionary process has stopped. Humans are transitional animals. We will disappear, as our countless ancestors have done. The badlands console me and reaffirm my belief in the sanctity of change and the perseverance of life.

The erosion-resistant cap rock on a hoodoo is the key factor in forming this characteristic badland landscape.

During a heavy rainstorm only a quarter of the rainfall soaks into the ground. Most of it flushes over the surface of the badlands, further eroding the slopes and gullies.

BADLANDS: WHAT, WHEN, WHERE, AND WHY?

A typical tract of badlands is all up and down. It consists of a landscape extensively dissected by steep, narrow valleys, the slopes of which are relatively free of vegetation, revealing multicolored layers of bedrock. Most of the bedrock that surfaces in the northern prairies, excluding the superficial glacial deposits, is sedimentary rock from the Cretaceous Period, 65 to 136 million years ago. During the late Cretaceous Period, a succession of large inland seas inundated the central basin of North America, including the northern mixed-grass prairies. At one point, this inland sea, called the Bearpaw Sea, stretched from the Arctic Ocean to the Gulf of Mexico. This immense sea finally disappeared about 65 million years ago with the general continental uplift of central North America. Over the millions of years of its existence, the size and shorelines of the Bearpaw Sea varied. Innumerable great rivers, laden with gravel, sands, silt, and clay from the uplands of the Canadian Shield in the east and the mountains in the west, emptied into the sea and dumped their cargo of sediments. The larger, heavier sediments settled first; later, they became compacted into conglomerates and coarse and fine sandstones. The fine clays and silts settled farther out from shore and became beds of siltstones and shales. Because of the nature of their deposition, all sedimentary rocks are layered, arranged in successive beds one on top of the other. If a sequence of beds has not been disturbed (by tectonic activity, for example), the layers at the bottom are the oldest, with increasingly younger layers on top. The rock layers differ in color and texture, depending upon the composition of the sediments and the parent rocks from which they originated.

During the Cretaceous, volcanoes occasionally erupted in areas west of the mixed-grassland region, spewing clouds of volcanic ash over the prairies. The ash was altered by weathering and transformed into bentonite, a clay with highly absorbent qualities.

Bentonite clay is found in a number of areas, and it is mined at Truax, in southern Saskatchewan, and in the Big Horn Basin of Wyoming. The clay has a diversity of uses, ranging from drilling muds to its inclusion as a bulking agent in cosmetics and toothpaste. Slopes containing bentonite are very slippery when wet, and the mud feels greasy or waxy. When it dries out, the surface cracks and forms characteristic crumbly chunks that resemble popcorn.

When you look at a chocolate layer cake, the icing is all you see before you remove a slice. The same applies to the sedimentary layers of bedrock that underlie the mixed-grass prairie. Unless something cuts into the bedrock, only the youngest layer on top is visible. The greatest enemy of rock is running water, and when rivers are laden with sediments, it adds to their bite, and the water eats into the bedrock. In the mixed grasslands, former glacial meltwater channels and rivers have cut deeply into the bedrock, exposing the layers of time and creating the badlands topography.

In Saskatchewan, badlands flank the Big Muddy, Moran, and Frenchman Rivers, and in Alberta, the shoulders of the Milk River valley have been sculpted into badlands that are like no others. Dramatic badlands flank the shoulders of the Missouri River in Montana, and in southwestern South Dakota, the rugged topography is celebrated in Badlands National Park. However, some of the most spectacular badlands parallel the banks of the Red Deer River, in Dinosaur Provincial Park in southern Alberta. In 1979, the park was selected as a World Heritage Site by the United Nations Educational, Scientific, and Cultural Organization (UNESCO) in recognition of its outstanding universal value as a dinosaur fossil field and as a landscape of unique physical character.

All badlands were created by the action of running water, and today the forces of erosion continue. The English language is full of expressions extolling the permanency of rock. Yet rocks everywhere, especially the relatively soft sedimentary rocks of the badlands, are slowly and continually dissolved by chemical action and attacked by wind-driven ice and grit that abrades their surfaces like sandpaper. The recurrent cycles of freezing and thawing can chip and fracture even the hardest rocks. But the true architect of erosion is water, as rain, runoff, hail, or sleet. Water expands 10 percent in volume when it freezes, and this expansion exerts an immense force within cracks. The products of all of this erosion are pinnacles, buttes, and hoodoos, the dramatic landforms of the badlands. These features prompted acclaimed artist A. Y. Jackson to praise the Red Deer badlands as "the most paintable landscape in western Canada."

The rock layers within the badlands vary in hardness and, thus, vary in their vulnerability to erosion. Harder layers persist longer, and sometimes when they overlie softer layers, hoodoos are formed. Hoodoos are mushroom-shaped pinnacles that typify the badlands. On a moonlit night, the hoodoos cast eerie shadows. Some Native American groups were frightened of hoodoos, believing them to be petrified giants who came alive at night and hurled rocks at intruders.

The forces of erosion are leveling the badlands, in Dinosaur Provincial Park, for example, by a centimeter (0.4 in.) a year. By geological standards, this is an exceptionally rapid rate of erosion. Compare it to the erosion rate in the Rocky Mountains—a centimeter every 1,000 years. One naturalist joked that in 10,000 years the badlands of Dinosaur Provincial Park would be flattened and she would be unemployed.

Erosion occurs not only on the surface of the badlands but also within them. Deep beneath the eroded slopes is a system of caves and piping channels. Scientists have released smoke bombs within the caves and watched where the smoke exits to determine the extensiveness of the underground network of channels. Thus, the badlands are being eaten away, inside and out, and carried away in rivers. After every rainfall, a little more of the slopes is washed away. The badlands originated from sediments washed in by extinct rivers, and now they are being washed away by today's rivers to form new beds of sediments that may, in millions of years, be exposed again. It is a recurrent cycle. But as the badlands are stripped away, fossils are exposed, and each year the agents of erosion deliver more remnants from the past for paleontologists to ponder.

THE PETRIFIED PAST

Webster's dictionary defines a fossil as "a remnant, impression, or trace of an animal or plant of past geological ages that has been preserved in the earth's crust." A fossil can be a footprint, the outline of a leaf, skin impressions, a bone or tooth, a shell, stomach stones, or petrified dung. Generally, if a structure is to become fossilized, it must first be rapidly buried by sediments. Then, groundwater slowly seeps into all of the cells and spaces of the buried material. Minerals, such as silica, calcite, and pyrite, that are present in the water slowly replace, molecule by molecule, the parts

Though few birds enliven the badlands in winter, it is a good time to see Nuttall's cottontails, mule deer, long-tailed weasels, and porcupines.

BEHOLD THE MIGHTY DINOSAUR

FAMOUS IN PREHISTORIC LORE,

NOT ONLY FOR HIS POWER AND STRENGTH

BUT FOR HIS INTELLECTUAL LENGTH.

YOU WILL OBSERVE BY THESE REMAINS

THE CREATURE HAD TWO SETS OF BRAINS -

ONE IN HIS HEAD (THE USUAL PLACE),

THE OTHER AT HIS SPINAL BASE.

THUS HE COULD REASON "A PRIORI"

AS WELL AS "A POSTERIORI."

NO PROBLEM BOTHERED HIM A BIT

HE MADE BOTH HEAD AND TAIL OF IT.

SO WISE WAS HE, SO WISE AND SOLEMN,

EACH THOUGHT FILLED JUST A SPINAL COLUMN.

IF ONE BRAIN FOUND THE PRESSURE STRONG

IT PASSED A FEW IDEAS ALONG.

IF SOMETHING SLIPPED HIS FORWARD MIND

'TWAS RESCUED BY THE ONE BEHIND.

AND IF IN ERROR HE WAS CAUGHT

HE HAD A SAVING AFTERTHOUGHT

AS HE THOUGHT TWICE BEFORE HE SPOKE

HE HAD NO JUDGEMENT TO REVOKE.

THUS HE COULD THINK WITHOUT CONGESTION

UPON BOTH SIDES OF EVERY QUESTION.

OH GAZE UPON THIS MODEL BEAST,

DEFUNCT 10 MILLION YEARS AT LEAST.

— BERT TAYLOR, *CHICAGO TRIBUNE*, 1912

Like all of the northern mixed-grass prairies, the badlands receive just 30–40 centimeters (12–16 in.) of precipitation per year, not much more than a desert.

of the wood, bone, or shell and form a replica of the original. At other times, the structure is simply buried quickly with sediment that solidifies and, later, when the original structure decomposes and disappears, a mold is left. The mold may then fill with minerals and a perfect cast is formed.

The most notable fossils to be found in the badlands are those of dinosaurs. The Age of Dinosaurs began about 200 million years ago in the middle of the Triassic Period, and dinosaurs flourished for about 130 million years. Dinosaurs were grazers, browsers, egg eaters, meat eaters, and scavengers; some were as small as today's iguanas, and others, such as Albertosaurus, were 15 meters (49 ft.) long and weighed more than a hundred people. A number of predatory dinosaurs walked upright on massive hind limbs. To supply these limbs with nerves, the terminal part of the animal's spinal cord was greatly enlarged—several times the size of its brain—and this led many to believe that the dinosaur had two brains.

Dinosaur remains have been found on every continent and, to date, at least four dozen species of dinosaurs have been uncovered from the Cretaceous deposits in the badlands of the mixed-grass prairies. At the end of the Cretaceous Period, the dinosaurs were flourishing in variety and in numbers, and then suddenly they were gone. Not one dinosaur skeleton has been found in the deposits of the Tertiary Period, which came after the Cretaceous Period.

THE DINOSAURS DISAPPEAR

Nothing can quite match the unfettered enthusiasm mustered by scientists in their early attempts to explain the extinction of the dinosaur. Overcrowding and a drop in global temperatures were popular theories. Competition from newly evolved mammals also seemed plausible, as did mammalian predation on dinosaur eggs. A few suggested that the newly evolving flowering plants of the late Cretaceous Period produced toxic alkaloids that poisoned the dinosaurs. But the most imaginative explanation is the one that postulates that flowering plants were indigestible to dinosaurs and they died of constipation.

The dinosaurs of the Cretaceous Period tended to be the largest of their kind. Greater size brought with it problems: slower movement, greater food requirements, and a longer period of development for the young. All of these factors make animals vulnerable to change, accident, and disease. The dinosaurs were not the only animals to suddenly disappear 65 million years ago. Seventy-five percent of all the animals and plants of the world disappeared along with the dinosaurs. Today, scientists believe they know how it happened.

Floating through space are countless fragments of rocks, remnants from the formation of the solar system. Scientists postulate that one of these fragments, an asteroid, traveling 65,000 kilometers per hour (40,000 MPH), collided with Earth in the region of the Yucatan Peninsula of Mexico. The asteroid, 10 kilometers (6 mi.) in diameter, would have vaporized on impact, throwing a dense dust cloud into the atmosphere and blocking out the sun. The cloud, swept along by the jet stream, would have quickly circled the planet. This theory is supported by a layer of clay found in rocks from the late Cretaceous Period in many parts of the world. The rocks contain unusual amounts of iridium, as much as 160 times the normal trace amounts. The chemical element iridium is rare in the rocks of our planet, but relatively abundant in asteroids. The asteroidal impact would have darkened the world for decades, possibly centuries, shutting down photosynthesis, disrupting plant growth, and collapsing the food chain. Plant-eating animals would have died first, followed by predators, and finally scavengers.

The records of the mass extinctions that ended the Cretaceous Period show certain anomalies. For example, land plants of the northern regions of the Temperate Zone suffered more losses than land plants farther south. But freshwater plants and animals of both northern and southern regions were scarcely affected. In another instance, no land animal weighing more than 25 kilograms (55 lb.) survived, yet many of the ones that disappeared were considerably smaller. The asteroidal impact theory answers many questions, but like any good detective story, it poses just as many.

OUTLAWS AND PILGRIMS
The badlands played a role in the lives of many people. In the 1880s, outlaw gangs lived in caves of the Big Muddy badlands of southern Saskatchewan and terrorized the region. At the time, a drought gripped the American prairies, and cattle died, ranches folded, and cowboys were set adrift, jobless and without a home. Many of these cowhands drifted north into the Montana-Saskatchewan country. Out of this migration sprang a tough, lawless gang of rowdies and rustlers called the Wild Bunch. The American West had Jesse James, Billy the Kid, and the Daltons, but the Wild Bunch included such notorious disreputables as

An abundance of prickly-pear cactuses is an indication that a prairie area is especially poor and dry, or is being over-grazed.

Dutch Henry, the Pigeon-Toed Kid, Bloody Knife, and the Nelson Gang, miscreants that all became legendary figures. Though train and bank robberies were included among their dastardly deeds, rustling livestock was the stock-in-trade of the Wild Bunch. The gang, hiding out in the Big Muddy, would regularly sneak across the border to steal horses and cattle. The livestock were herded back across the border into Canada, the brands "adjusted," and the animals sold. These same animals were often stolen again and taken back to the Dakotas and Montana to be sold once more. The ranchers on both sides of the border were threatened continually, and they lived in constant fear of reprisals.

Befitting their lifestyle, many of the Wild Bunch gang came to a colorful end. Bloody Knife was killed in a drunken brawl, and an angry posse convinced the Pigeon-Toed Kid to hang around for a while. Others were shot by American lawmen or ended their days in prison cells. Sam Kelly, believed to be the leader of the gang, died in North Battleford, Saskatchewan, in 1954, alone and in obscurity.

For the Native Americans of the plains, the badlands were a sacred place. The Natives believed that the world was charged with supernatural importance and that all natural phenomena—mountains, rivers, waterfalls, and cliffs—were manifestations of sacred spirits. It is easy to understand how the sculpted valleys and hoodoos of the badlands acquired a reputation as a place of powerful spirits.

Writing-On-Stone Provincial Park in the Milk River badlands of southern Alberta is the site of one of the largest collections of prehistoric rock art in North America. Thousands of petroglyphs, and a few

The ferruginous hawk is the largest and heaviest hawk in the prairies. This one was defending a dead ground squirrel.

The intense blue of the mountain bluebird is not due to the presence of pigments. Rather, it is an optical illusion caused by the microscopic structure of the bird's feathers.

rock paintings, petrographs, grace the golden sandstone badlands of the park. The Aboriginal artwork depicts men with shields and weapons, elk, bison, bears, horses, snakes, and birds. The area has been part of the religious beliefs and practices of Native peoples for over 3,000 years. For them, the badlands were a holy place to be respected and feared, where spirits wrote on the rocks. Native warriors came to Writing-On-Stone to seek advice from their guardian spirits. Before entering the valley they would select a high point, build a fire of sweet grass (*Hierochloe odorata*), and inhale the smoke to purify themselves. Afterward, they would fast for days and in their dreams receive inspiration, and perhaps also learn of the future. A person could add his own inscriptions, but only if he received instructions in a vision. The visions contained secret knowledge from which the dreamer obtained his power.

Rock art is found in other mixed-grassland regions: in Saskatchewan near Estevan and Assiniboia and in Montana near Billings. The Plains Natives believed that the acts of carving and painting were a means of acquiring power and regaining control over their environment, and since they were subject to the vicissitudes of nature, such beliefs may have been their only defence against despair. Like most people today, the Native Americans of the prairies were sustained by their faith.

GREAT BALLS OF SNAKES
Snakes cannot withstand prolonged freezing, so in the northern prairies where winter temperatures may plummet to -40 degrees Centigrade (-40 degrees F.), they hibernate underground for six or seven months every year. In the badlands, they seek refuge below the

frost line in deep crevices and piping systems. Different species may sometimes use the same den: garter snakes (*Thamnophis* spp.), yellow-bellied racers (*Coluber constrictor*), bullsnakes (*Pituophis catenifer*), and prairie rattlesnakes. Since snakes evolved in the tropics, their survival in a seasonally cold climate such as the northern prairies is a challenge. The red-sided garter snake (*Thamnophis sirtalis parietalis*), a widespread prairie species, ranges farther north than any other snake in North America. In the past thirty years, the study of this snake has shed light on how some reptiles adapt to cold environments.

Typically, the red-sided garter snake, like many prairie snakes, overwinters in communal dens, but none of the others does it on such a grand scale as they do. As many as 10,000 garter snakes may share the same winter den—the largest aggregation of snakes anywhere on the planet. Throughout the winter, the snakes clump together in the darkened depths of the den where temperatures hover around the freezing point. The warmth of spring lures them to the surface. Male garter snakes, pencil thin from months of fasting, are the first to appear, emerging together in great numbers. Hundreds, and even thousands, may surface at once. Soon afterward, over a period of several weeks, the females emerge, one by one or in small groups. The staggered, delayed emergence of female garter snakes as opposed to the early, mass emergence of the males may have survival value. With the ratio of males to females around the den entrance as high as 50 to 1, the probability of a female being fertilized is virtually 100 percent. Also important to consider is that if all the females were to emerge together, mate,

and disperse early in the season, unpredictable freezing temperatures might destroy much of the breeding population. The intermittent emergence of the females insures that some will survive.

As each female appears at the surface, she is mobbed by male suitors. "Mating balls" are formed, consisting

A trio of male red-sided garter snakes court the thick body of a female. As many as one hundred males may mob a receptive female.

During the spring mating season Nuttall's cottontails cuff each other in the face and ears. Surprisingly, females do most of the clouting, and the rabbits they clout are courting males.

of a single female intertwined with as many as a hundred males, each intent on copulation. The female is cold and torpid when she first emerges, and her sluggishness probably works to the advantage of the courting males. An odor chemical, called a *pheromone*, detectable in the skin of the female's back, advertises her sex and her readiness for mating. The males flick their tongues rapidly over her back, sensing the tantalizing taste.

Copulation in red-sided garter snakes lasts fifteen to twenty minutes. The males possess two copulatory organs, called *hemipenes*—hollow, cylindrical bodies that retract into cavities in the base of the snake's tail. Just one hemipenis is used in a mating. Afterward, the male deposits a gelatinous plug in the female's cloaca, as a kind of biological chastity belt. As well, mating secretions produced by the male and/or the female are smeared around her cloacal region, leaving a shiny coating. The secretions contain a second pheromone, a sexual repellent, which renders mated females unattractive and dissuades courting males. Thus, once females are mated, they are spared the continued harassment by amorous males at a time when their energy reserves are especially low. Most females mate within thirty minutes and leave the den area soon afterward to disperse to summer feeding marshes where the young will be born in late August.

In recent years, inquisitive researchers have discovered yet another twist to the fascinating biology of the red-sided garter snake. Surprisingly, some males, when they first emerge, exude the seductive pheromones of a female, and they are vigorously mobbed and courted by regular males. These mixed-up males, called "she-males," still behave like regular males and have a lusty appetite for females; they just smell different. In fact, a female-hunting she-male may smell so good that he falls in love with himself. If a she-male should accidentally tongue-test his own tail amidst a tangle of tails, he may spend considerable time courting himself! Researchers are uncertain why a small percentage of male garter snakes mimic females. Perhaps it fools rival males and diverts their attention from real females, thus improving the she-male's chances of mating. Whatever the reason, we can expect to be surprised by this fascinating reptile.

Life in the cold prairies influences the biology of the garter snake in one final way. Most prairie snakes lay eggs, but garter snakes give birth to live young. The mother garter snake retains her fifteen to thirty eggs inside her body throughout their development, and each time she basks, the eggs are warmed and incubated, improving their odds of survival. The prairie rattlesnake follows the same strategy of bearing live young, likely for the same reason. When other species of snakes lay eggs, the eggs are usually left to develop on their own and are vulnerable to destruction by cold summer weather, something that occurs frequently on the northern prairies.

THE BLACK WIDOW

Within a day of her capture in July 1983, the female black widow spider had spun a disorganized sheet of webbing inside the empty peanut butter jar where I kept her. She spent her time hanging beneath the web, the scarlet hourglass on her ebony abdomen advertising her identity. Kilogram for kilogram, she was the most dangerous animal I had ever photographed. I knew that no one in Canada had ever died from the bite of a black

Little is known about the biology of the northern scorpion, an uncommon and secretive resident of the prairie badlands.

widow spider, but I wasn't sure if the spider knew that, and having her as a pet was an exhilarating experience. One morning, her abdomen was markedly shrunken and she had spun a globular, silken egg case. For weeks after that, she was always beside her eggs, leaving them only to feed on the dead house flies I provided her. On 17 August, five weeks after her capture, there was a tiny hole in the egg sac, and the web was sprinkled with forty-nine brown-and-white spiderlings. In the wild, adult females die shortly after their eggs hatch, and the young disperse to spend the winter alone. My spiders now live in drawer No. 674 of the invertebrate collection of the Saskatchewan Museum of Natural History in Regina. They were the first black widow spiders collected in the province.

The western black widow spider (*Latrodectus hesperus*) is found throughout the arid grasslands, from southern Alberta and southwestern Saskatchewan to Arizona and New Mexico. In the northern prairies, they commonly build their webs in the cavities of badlands and in deserted burrows of red foxes, badgers, and ground squirrels. In Alberta, in the summer of 2002, I found three black widows, each in a separate burrow, within 50 meters (164 ft.) of the active nest of a burrowing owl.

Male black widows are much smaller than adult females (about ¹⁄₁₀th the size) and are not black, but patterned with gray, tan, and orange. Some authorities claim the males are just as venomous as the females, but their small fangs make it difficult for them to pierce a human's skin except where it is thin, such as around the genitals—a theory I have no interest in testing. Prior to mating, the male spider spins a tiny sperm web upon which he deposits a globule of semen. The copulatory organs of a spider look like boxing gloves at the end of two short, leglike appendages located beside the spider's head. The male dips his boxing gloves, called *pedipalps,* into the globule of semen and fills them with sperm. He is now ready to look for a date.

Unlike the wolf spider (Family Lycosidae), which uses vision to locate both its mate and its prey, the black widow is a web builder and relies on web vibrations to signal the approach of a prospective suitor. The male spider cautiously approaches the edge of the female's web and plucks out a vibratory message to identify himself to her. The predacious nature of spiders makes recognition of the sexual partner especially important. The strands of the black widow's web contain a pheromone that identifies her to the male. If she is receptive, the male maneuvers his pedipalps next to the genital openings on the underside of her abdomen, and sperm is transferred. Afterward, the male usually, but not always, lingers on the female's web, and she eats him. The common name "black widow" refers to this interesting reproductive strategy. If the male spider were not eaten, it would normally die soon after mating anyway. By consuming her mate, the female black widow gains vital nutrients to provision her eggs. The male also benefits because the nourished female may now produce more eggs and, thus, more copies of his genes.

HOT ENOUGH TO FRY AN EGG

Shrubby vegetation is scanty over much of the badlands, with clumps of creeping juniper, greasewood (*Sarcobatus vermiculatus*), rabbitbrush (*Chrysothamnus nauseosus*), and sagebrush (*Artemisia cana*) scattered here and there. Grasses and clusters of western snowberry and prairie rose (*Rosa arkansana*) grow in the bottoms of ravines, where runoff provides more moisture. For the most part, however, the badlands are naked slopes of clay and sandstone that shimmer in the summer heat. I sometimes carry a thermometer when I hike, and once, when I placed it on a clay slope in the badlands, the mercury went past 50 degrees Centigrade (122 degrees F.) and off the end of the scale. The clay slopes of the badlands are a harsh, demanding habitat—the ultimate test of animal adaptability. Dozens of species of birds nest in the badlands, but only two, the common nighthawk (*Chordeiles minor*) and the common poorwill (*Phalaenoptilus nuttallii*), regularly make their nests on bare ground in the open where unprotected eggs can fry within minutes.

Both birds protect their eggs on hot, bare ground by incubating them constantly, so the temperature of the eggs stays the same as the parent's body temperature, even when air temperatures climb. While incubating, parent nighthawks and poorwills run the risk of becoming overheated. Like all birds, they must maintain their body temperature within fairly strict limits, roughly between 36 and 43 degrees Centigrade (97 and 110 degrees F.). The reflective properties of their plumage lessen the risk somewhat, but both birds rely on evaporation from the linings of their mouths to cool themselves. And one thing these birds have is a big mouth. Despite their tiny beaks, the nighthawk and the poorwill have an enormous gape that opens up as far back as their ears. In the nighthawk, the bird's mouth is equal to 15 percent of its total body area. So, as soon as the birds begin to overheat, they simply open their

mouth, and there is a large, moist surface over which evaporation can occur. The lining of their mouth is especially rich in blood vessels, which further helps to dissipate body heat.

An ingenious experiment showed that the adult nighthawk, and possibly also the poorwill, treats

A female black widow may move her silken egg sac in and out of the sun throughout the day to control the temperature of the eggs inside.

The cryptic plumage of a common nighthawk chick blends well with the weathered clay slopes of the badlands.

The average nest of a cliff swallow consists of 900 to 1200 mud pellets and takes a pair a week or two to construct. The finished nest will be roughly the size of a cantaloupe.

its eggs as extensions of its own body. In the study, the nighthawk's two eggs were replaced with plastic replicas, each containing a heating coil. When the investigators increased the temperature of the artificial eggs, the adult bird responded by opening its mouth and panting, using the same cooling behavior it uses to protect its own body from overheating.

The nighthawk and poorwill are insect-eating birds that belong to a group called the *caprimulgids*, which is Latin for goatsucker. The legendary Greek philosopher and scientist Aristotle wrote of the caprimulgids:

"Flying to the udder of she-goats, it sucks them, and thus gets its name." The ancients believed that under the cover of darkness these birds latched onto the udders of goats and sheep and milked the animals dry. Actually, the birds swooped around livestock to snatch insects flushed from the grass by the animals. Besides, the stomach of a goatsucker is barely the size of a thimble so it would take quite a flock of them to milk a goat dry, let alone convince the irascible old nanny to stand still while all this was happening.

The short-horned lizard is a sit-and-wait predator that feeds on small insects, mainly ants and beetles.

FURTHER READING

INTRODUCTION

Barbour, Michael G., and William Dwight Billings, eds. *North American Terrestrial Vegetation.* New York: Cambridge University Press, 1988.

Bolen, Eric G. *Ecology of North America.* New York: John Wiley & Sons Inc., 1998.

Coupland, R. T., and R. T. Brayshaw. "The Fescue Grassland in Saskatchewan." *Ecology* 53 (1953): 475–507.

Cushman, Ruth Carol, and Stephen R. Jones. *The Shortgrass Prairie.* Boulder, CO: Pruett Publishing Company, 1988.

Duncan, P. *Tallgrass Prairie—The Inland Sea.* Kansas City, KS: Lowell Press, 1979.

Lynch, Wayne. *Wild Birds Across the Prairies.* Calgary, AB: Fifth House Ltd., 1999.

Sibley, David Allen. *The Sibley Guide to Birds.* New York: Alfred A. Knopf, 2000.

Vance, F. R., J. R. Jowsey, and J. S. McLean. *Wildflowers Across the Prairies.* 2ᵈ ed. Vancouver, BC: Greystone Books, 1993.

Wilson, Don E., and Sue Ruff, eds. *The Smithsonian Book of North American Mammals.* Washington, DC: Smithsonian Institution Press, 1999.

THE LAND: ITS FACE AND ITS TEMPERAMENT

Ammerman, A. J. "Late Pleistocene Population Dynamics: An Alternative View." *Human Ecology* 4 (1975): 219–233.

Anonymous. *Potash in Canada.* Ottawa, ON: Government of Canada, Energy, Mines and Resources, 1978.

Bambach, R., and A. M. Ziegler. "Before Pangea: The Geographies of the Paleozoic World." *American Scientist* 68, No. 2 (1980): 48–60.

Beatty, C. *Landscapes of Southern Alberta.* Lethbridge, AB: University of Lethbridge Production Series, 1975.

Bielstein, H. U. *Coal Resources and Reserves of Canada.* Ottawa, ON: Ministry of Supply and Services, 1980.

Bryson, R. "Ancient Climes on the Great Plains." *Natural History* (July 1980): 65–73.

Carder, A. C. "Climate and Rangelands of Canada." *Journal of Range Management* 23 (1970): 263–67.

Courtillot, V., and G. Vink. "How Continents Break Up." *Scientific American* (July 1983): 43–49.

Covey, C. "The Earth's Orbit and Ice Ages." *Scientific American* 250, No. 2 (1984): 55–66.

Decker, Robert, and Barbara Decker. *Volcanoes.* 2ᵈ ed. New York: W. H. Freeman and Company, 1989.

Duxbury, Alyn C., and Alison B. Duxbury. *An Introduction to the World's Oceans.* 4ᵗʰ ed. Dubuque, Iowa: Wm. C. Brown Publishers, 1994.

Flannery, Tim. *The Eternal Frontier—An Ecological History of North America and Its Peoples.* New York: Atlantic Monthly Press, 2001.

Kurten, Bjorn, and Elaine Anderson. *Pleistocene Mammals of North America.* New York: Columbia University Press, 1980.

Lister, Adrian, and Paul Bahn. *Mammoths.* New York: Macmillan, 1994.

Phillips, David. *The Climates of Canada.* Ottawa, ON: Ministry of Supply and Services, 1990.

Pielou, E. C. *After the Ice Age—The Return of Life to Glaciated North America.* Chicago, IL: University of Chicago Press, 1991.

Ritchie, J. C. "The Late Quaternary Vegetational History of the Western Interior of Canada." *Canadian Journal of Botany* 54, No. 15 (1976): 1793–1818.

Stearn, C., Robert L. Carroll, and Thomas H. Clark. *Geological Evolution of North America.* 3ʳᵈ ed. Toronto, ON: John Wiley & Sons, 1979.

Stegner, Wallace. *Wolf Willow.* New York: Viking Press, 1966.

THE LEVEL PLAINS: FLAT ALL YEAR ROUND

Barth, Friedrich G. *Insects and Flowers—The Biology of a Partnership.* Princeton, NJ: Princeton University Press, 1991.

Bartos, D. L., and P. L. Sims. "Root Dynamics of a Shortgrass Ecosystem." *Journal of Range Management* 27, No. 1 (1974): 33–36.

Best, K. F., and J. Looman. *Prairie Grasses.* Ottawa, ON: Canada Agriculture, Publication No. 1413, 1971.

Byers, John A. *American Pronghorn—Social Adaptations and the Ghosts of Predators Past.* Chicago, IL: University of Chicago Press, 1997.

Coupland, R. T. "Ecology of the Mixed Prairie in Canada." *Ecological Monograph* 20, No. 4 (1950): 271–316.

Coupland, R. T., and R. E. Johnson. "Rooting Characteristics of Native Grassland Species in Saskatchewan." *Journal of Ecology* 53 (1965): 475–507.

Epp, H. T. "Prehistoric Human-Bison Ecology on the Plains." *Napao* 1, No. 1 (1968): 40–47.

Ernst, Carl H. *Venomous Reptiles of North America.* Washington, DC: Smithsonian Institution Press, 1992.

Finnigan, J. T. *Tipi Rings and Plains Prehistory: A Reassessment of their Archeological Potential.* Ottawa, ON: National Museum of Canada, Mercury Series No. 108, 1982.

Gill, Frank B. *Ornithology.* 2ᵈ ed. New York: W. H. Freeman and Company, 1995.

Holldobler, Bert, and Edward O. Wilson. *The Ants.* Cambridge, MA: Harvard University Press, 1990.

Hoogland, John L. *The Black-tailed Prairie Dog—Social Life of a Burrowing Mammal.* Chicago, IL: University of Chicago Press, 1995.

Johnsgard, Paul A. *Grouse of the World.* Lincoln, NB: University of Nebraska Press, 1983.

———. *Prairie Birds—Fragile Splendor in the Great Plains.* Lawrence, KS: University Press of Kansas, 2001.

———. *Grassland Grouse and Their Conservation.* Washington, DC: Smithsonian Institution Press, 2002.

———. *Owls of North America.* 2ᵈ ed. Washington, DC: Smithsonian Institution Press, 2002.

Kehoe, T. F. *Indian Boulder Effigies.* Regina, SK: Saskatchewan Museum of Natural History, Popular Series No. 12, 1976.

Klauber, Lawrence M. *Rattlesnakes—Their Habits, Life Histories, and Influence on Mankind.* Los Angeles, CA: University of California Press, 1972.

Kurten, Bjorn, and Elaine Anderson. *Pleistocene Mammals of North America.* New York: Columbia University Press, 1980.

Langer, R. M. *How Grasses Grow.* Institute of Biology's Studies in Biology, No. 34. London, UK: Edward Arnold, 1972.

Lowther, P. E. "Brown-headed Cowbird (*Molothrus ater*)." In *The Birds of North America,* edited by A. Poole and F. Gill, No. 47. Philadelphia, PA: The Academy of Natural Sciences; Washington, DC: The American Ornithologists' Union, 1993.

Lynch, Wayne. *Wild Birds Across the Prairies.* Calgary, AB: Fifth House Ltd., 1999.

Reeves, B. O. K. *Cultural Change in the Northern Plains: 1000 B.C. to A.D. 1000.* Edmonton, AB: Archeological Survey of Alberta, Occasional Paper No. 20, Alberta Culture, 1983.

Rowe, Matthew P., Richard G. Coss, and Donald H. Owings. "Rattlesnake Rattles and Burrowing Owl Hisses: A Case of Acoustic Batesian Mimicry." *Ethology* 72 (1986): 53–71.

Welty, Joel Carl, and Luis Baptista. *The Life of Birds.* 4ᵗʰ ed. New York: Saunders College Publishing, 1988.

Young, James A. "Tumbleweed." *Scientific American* (March 1991): 82–87.

SAND HILLS: PRAIRIE WINDSCAPES

Best, K. F., and J. Looman. *Prairie Grasses.* Ottawa, ON: Canada Agriculture, Publication No. 1413, 1971.

Chase, J. D., W. E. Howard, and J. T. Roseberry. "Pocket Gophers."

In *Wild Mammals of North America,* edited by J. A. Chapman and C. A. Feldhamer, 239–55. Baltimore, MD: Johns Hopkins University Press, 1982.

Connelly, J. W., M. W. Gratson, and K. P. Reese. "Sharp-tailed Grouse (*Tympanuchus phasianellus*)." In *The Birds of North America,* edited by A. Poole and F. Gill, No. 354. Philadelphia, PA: The Birds of North America Inc., 1998.

Epp, H. T., and L. Townley-Smith, eds. *The Great Sand Hills of Saskatchewan.* Regina, SK: Saskatchewan Department of the Environment, 1980.

Garrison, Tom E., and Troy L. Best. *Dipodomys ordii.* Mammalian Species No. 353. Provo, UT: The American Society of Mammalogists, 1990.

Geist, Valerius. *Mule Deer Country.* Saskatoon, SK: Western Producer Prairie Books, 1990.

———. *Deer of the World—Their Evolution, Behavior, and Ecology.* Mechanicsburg, PA: Stackpole Books, 1998.

Gummer, D. L. *Ord's Kangaroo Rat (Dipodomys ordii).* Edmonton, AB: Alberta Environmental Protection, Wildlife Management Division, Wildlife Status Report No. 4, 1997.

Krupa, J. J. "*Bufo cognatus.* Great Plains Toad." *Catalogue of American Amphibians and Reptiles* (1990): 457.1–457.8.

Lacey, Eileen A., James L. Patton, and Guy N. Cameron. *Life Underground—The Biology of Subterranean Rodents.* Chicago, IL: University of Chicago Press, 2000.

Lofts, B. *Animal Photoperiodism.* Institute of Biology's Studies in Biology, No. 25. London, UK: Edward Arnold, 1970.

Platt, D. R. "Natural History of the Hognose Snakes, *Heterodon playrhinos* and *Heterodon nascius.*" *University of Kansas Museum of Natural History Publication* 18, no. 4 (1969): 253–420.

Reynolds, J. A., and C. M. Stevens. "Footdrumming and Other Anti-predator Responses in the Banner-tailed Kangaroo Rat (*Dipodomys spectabilis*)." *Behavioural Ecology and Sociobiology* 20 (1987):187–94.

Russell, Anthony P., and Aaron M. Bauer. *The Amphibians and Reptiles of Alberta - A Field Guide and Primer of Boreal Herpetology.* 2ᵈ ed. Calgary, AB: University of Calgary Press, 2000.

Stebbins, Robert C., and Nathan Cohen. *A Natural History of Amphibians.* Princeton, NJ: Princeton University Press, 1995.

Wallmo, O. C., ed. *Mule and Black-tailed Deer of North America.* Lincoln, NB: University of Nebraska Press, 1981.

Wilson, Don E., and Sue Ruff, eds. *The Smithsonian Book of North American Mammals.* Washington, DC: Smithsonian Institution Press, 1999.

COULEES: VALLEYS OF DISCOVERY

Bryan, Liz. *The Buffalo People—Prehistoric Archeology on the Canadian Plains*. Edmonton, AB: University of Alberta Press, 1991.

Fenton, M. B., and J. H. Fullard. "Moth Hearing and Feeding Strategies of Bats." *American Scientist* 69 (1981): 266–75.

Fenton, M. Brock. *Bats*. New York: Checkmark Books, 2001.

Foster, John, Dick Harrison, and I. S. MacLaren, eds. *Buffalo*. Alberta Nature and Culture Series. Edmonton, AB: University of Alberta Press, 1992.

Geist, Valerius. *Buffalo Nation—History and Legend of the North American Bison*. Calgary, AB: Fifth House Publishers, 1996.

Hill, John E., and James D. Smith. *Bats—A Natural History*. Austin, TX: University of Texas Press, 1984.

Houston, C. S., D. G. Smith, and C. Rohner. "Great Horned Owl (*Bubo virginianus*)." In *The Birds of North America*, edited by A. Poole and F. Gill, No. 372. Philadelphia, PA: The Birds of North America Inc., 1998.

Lehane, M. J. *Biology of Blood-Sucking Insects*. London, UK: Harper Collins Academic, 1991.

Lott, Dale F. *American Bison—A Natural History*. Berkley, CA: University of California Press, 2002.

Marks, J. S., D. L. Evans, and D. W. Holt. "Long-eared Owl (*Asio otus*)." In *The Birds of North America*, edited by A. Poole and F. Gill, No. 133. Philadelphia, PA: The Birds of North America Inc., 1994.

Martin, Graham. *Birds by Night*. London, UK: T & A D Poyser, 1990.

Preston-Mafham, Rod and Ken. *Encyclopedia of Land Invertebrate Behaviour*. London, UK: Blandford Books, 1993.

Ruppert, Edward E., and Robert D. Barnes. *Invertebrate Zoology*. 6th ed. New York: Saunders College Publishing, 1994.

Waldbauer, Gilbert. *Insects Through the Seasons*. Cambridge, MA: Harvard University Press, 1996.

Wilson, Don E., and Sue Ruff, eds. *The Smithsonian Book of North American Mammals*. Washington, DC: Smithsonian Institution Press, 1999.

SLOUGHS: WATER AND WINGS

Alerstam, Thomas. *Bird Migration*. Cambridge, UK: Cambridge University Press, 1990.

Berthold, Peter. *Bird Migration—A General Survey*. Oxford, UK: Oxford University Press, 1993.

Cullen, S. A., J. R. Jehl, Jr., and G. L. Nuechterlein. "Eared Grebe (*Podiceps nigricollis*)." In *The Birds of North America*, edited by A. Poole and F. Gill, No. 433. Philadelphia, PA: The Birds of North America Inc., 1999.

Duellman, William E., and Linda Trueb. *Biology of Amphibians*. New York: McGraw Hill Book Co., 1986.

England, A. S., M. J. Bechard, and C. S. Houston. "Swainson's Hawk (*Buteo swainsoni*)." In *The Birds of North America*, edited by A. Poole and F. Gill, No. 265. Philadelphia, PA: The Birds of North America Inc., 1997.

Hotchkiss, Neil. *Common Marsh, Underwater and Floating-leaved Plants of the United States and Canada*. New York: Dover Publications Inc., 1972.

Johnsgard, Paul A. *Diving Birds of North America*. Lincoln, NB: University of Nebraska Press, 1987.

Lehane, M. J. *Biology of Blood-Sucking Insects*. London, UK: Harper Collins Academic, 1991.

Lynch, Wayne. *Wild Birds Across the Prairies*. Calgary, AB: Fifth House Ltd., 1999.

Muller, M. J., and R. W. Storer. "Pied-billed Grebe (*Podilymbus podiceps*)." In *The Birds of North America*, edited by A. Poole and F. Gill, No. 410. Philadelphia, PA: The Birds of North America Inc., 1999.

Novak, Milan, James A. Baker, Martyn E. Obbard, and Bruce Malloch, eds. *Wild Furbearer Management and Conservation in North America*. Toronto, ON: Ministry of Natural Resources, 1987.

Palmer, Ralph S., ed. *Handbook of North American Birds, Volume 2 (Waterfowl Part 1) & 3 (Waterfowl Part 2)*. Hartford, CT: Yale University Press, 1976.

Poulin, R. G., S. D. Grindal, and R. M. Brigham. "Common Nighthawk (*Chordeiles minor*)." In *The Birds of North America*, edited by A. Poole and F. Gill, No. 213. Philadelphia, PA: The Birds of North America Inc., 1996.

Russell, Anthony P., and Aaron M. Bauer. *The Amphibians and Reptiles of Alberta—A Field Guide and Primer of Boreal Herpetology*. 2d ed. Calgary, AB: University of Calgary Press, 2000.

Sowls, L. K. *Prairie Ducks*. Harrisburg, PA: Stackpole Books, 1955.

Spielman, Andrew, and Michael D'Antonio. *Mosquito—The Story of Man's Deadliest Foe*. New York: Hyperion, 2001.

Stedman, S. J. "Horned Grebe (*Podiceps auritus*)." In *The Birds of North America*, edited by A. Poole and F. Gill, No. 505. Philadelphia, PA: The Birds of North America Inc., 2000.

Van Der Valk, Arnold, ed. *Northern Prairie Wetlands*. Ames, IA: Iowa State University, 1989.

BADLANDS: LAYERS OF TIME

Csada, R. D., and R. M. Brigham. "Common Poorwill." In *The Birds of North America*, edited by A. Poole, P. Stettenheim, and

F. Gill, No. 32. Philadelphia, PA: The Birds of North America Inc., 1992.

Dawkins, Richard. *The Selfish Gene*. New ed. New York: Oxford University Press, 1989.

Foelix, Ranier F. *The Biology of Spiders*. Cambridge, MA: Harvard University Press, 1982.

Gertsch, Willis J. *American Spiders*. 2ᵈ ed. New York: Van Nostrand Reinhold Company, 1979.

Gregory, P. T. "Life-history Parameters of the Red-sided Garter Snake (*Thamnophis sirtalis sirtalis*) in an extreme environment, the Interlake Region of Manitoba." *National Museum of Canada Publication Zoology* 13 (1977):1–44.

Leech, Robin, and Maja Laird. "Egg Sac Incubation and Related Activities by the Black Widow Spider, *Latrodectus hesperus*, in Alberta, with notes on other species (Arachnidae: Araneida)." *Alberta Naturalist.* 13, No. 3 (1983):106–9.

Lynch, Wayne. "Great Balls of Snakes." *Natural History* (April 1983): 64–69.

Mason, R. T. "Chemical Ecology of the Red-sided Garter Snake, *Thamnophis sirtalis parietails.*" *Brain, Behaviour and Evolution.* 41 (1993): 261–68.

Poulin, R. G., S. D. Grindal, and R. M. Brigham. "Common Nighthawk (*Chordeiles minor*)." In *The Birds of North America*, edited by A. Poole and F. Gill, No. 213. Philadelphia, PA: The Birds of North America Inc., 1996.

Shine, R., and R. Mason. "Serpentine Cross-dressers." *Natural History* (February 2001): 56–61.

INDEX

Page numbers appearing in bold indicate photographs.

short-eared (*Asio flammeus*) **iv–v**, 78; snowy (*Nyctea scandiaca*) **58**

P

Panthera leo (lion) 22, 47
Pica hudsonia (American magpie) 37
Phalaenoptilus nuttallii (common poorwill) 127, 129
Photoperiod 56–58
Pipit, Sprague's (*Anthus spragueii*) 37
Pituophis catenifer (bullsnake) **109**, 123
Plate tectonics 10
Pocket gopher, northern (*Thomomys talpoides*) 63–64, **64**
Poplar, aspen (*Populus tremuloides*) **13**, 54
Populus tremuloides (aspen poplar) **13**, 54
Porcupine (*Erethizon dorsatum*) 51, **65**
Poorwill, common (*Phalaenoptilus nuttallii*) 127, 129
Prairie-chicken, greater (*Tympanuchus cupido*) **39**, 56
Prairie dog, black-tailed (*Cynomys ludovicianus*) 42, 44–45
Pronghorn (*Antilocapra americana*) 2, 46–48, **48–49**
Prunus virginiana (red chokecherry) 4
Pseudacris maculata (boreal chorus frog) 89, 95
Puccinella nuttalliana (alkali grass) 54

R

Rattlesnake, prairie (*Crotalus viridis viridis*) 7, 42, **45**, 45–46, 60
Recurvirostra americana (American avocet) 87, **104**

Rocky Mountains 12, 16, 24
Russian thistle, See Tumbleweed

S

Sagebrush (*Artemisia* spp.) **viii–ix**, 4, 55, 126
Salamander, tiger (*Ambystoma tigrinum*) 89, **95**
Salsola kali (tumbleweed) **13**, 34
Saskatchewan 16, 19, 24, 45, 49, 52, 58, 73, 86, 115, 120
Saskatoon (*Amelanchier alnifolia*) 4, 82
Skunk, striped (*Mephitis mephitis*) 37, 41, 78
Snake: red-sided garter (*Thamnophis sirtalis parietalis*) **123**,123–125; western hognose (*Heterdon nascius*) 61, **61**
Snowberry, western (*Symphoricarpos occidentalis*) 4
South Dakota 13, 25, 73, 86, 112, 115
Spea bombifrons (plains spadefoot toad) 55, **60**, 60–62, 95
Spermophilus richardsonii (Richardson's ground squirrel) **5**, 42, **43**, 63
Spiders: 62–63; western black widow (*Latrodectus hesperus*) 125–126, **127**
Sporobolus cryptandrus (sand dropseed) 55
Stipa comata (needle-and-thread grass) 3, 35
Stipa spartea (porcupine grass) 35
Sturnella neglecta (western meadowlark) 37, **38**
Sweetgrass Hills Montana **31**, 100–101
Symphoricarpos occidentalis (western snowberry) 4

T

Taxidea taxus (American badger) 41, **44**, 56, 59
Tepee ring **22–23**, 48
Texas 30
Thamnophis sirtalis parietalis (red-sided garter snake) **123**, 123–125
Thermopsis rhombifolia (golden-bean) **33**
Thomomys talpoides (northern pocket gopher) 63–64, **64**
Tick, wood (*Dermacentor andersoni*) 5, 70–72
Toad: Great Plains (Bufo *cognatus*) 55, 95; plains spadefoot (*Spea bombifrons*) 55, 60, 60–62, 95
Tumbleweed (S*alsola kali*) **13**, 34
Turkey, wild (Meleagris *gallopavo*) 71
Tympanuchus cupido (greater prairie-chicken) **39**, 56
Tympanuchus phasianellus (sharp-tailed grouse) 55, **55**, 56

V

Vulpes vulpes (red fox) **77**

W

Water striders 93, 94
Wyoming 24, 49, 52, 73, 115

X

Xanthocephalus xanthocephalus (yellow-headed blackbird) **86**, 86

ABOUT FIFTH HOUSE

FIFTH HOUSE PUBLISHERS, a Fitzhenry & Whiteside company, is a proudly Western Canadian press. Our publishing specialty is non-fiction as we believe that every community must possess a positive understanding of its worth and place if it is to remain vital and progressive. Fifth House is committed to "bringing the West to the rest" by publishing approximately twenty books a year about the land and people who make this region unique. Our books are selected for their quality, saleability, interest to readers, and contribution to the understanding of Western Canadian (and Canadian) history, culture, and environment.

Look for the following Fifth House titles by Wayne Lynch at your favorite bookstore:

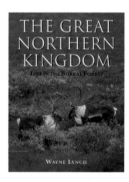

The Great Northern Kingdom: Life in the Boreal Forest

Hardcover $39.^{95} (CDN), $29.^{95} (U.S.)

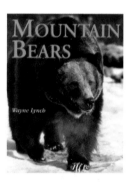

Mountain Bears

Paperback $15.^{95} (CDN), $14.^{95} (U.S.)

The Scoop on Poop! The Fascinating Science of How Animals Use Poop

Paperback $8.^{95} (CDN), $6.^{95} (U.S.)
Hardcover $18.^{95} (CDN), $11.^{95} (U.S.)

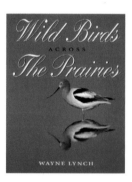

Wild Birds Across the Prairies

Paperback $24.^{95} (CDN), $18.^{95} (U.S.)

(prices subject to change)